A Taste of the Isle

Family Recipes Celebrating Manx P

The Friends of Laxey School
would like to thank all our sponsors and those who volunteered their invaluable
help in the publication of this book - all recipe contributors, Laxey School staff, Laxey
School pupils, Fols committee members, Adrian Cain and the Manx Heritage
Foundation, Peter Whittaker at Crowes, photographers Richard Kinley and Sarah
Henthorn, Isle of Man Newspapers, recipe checkers, patient husbands - and anyone
else who helped transform a germ of an idea into a project with a passion!

All proceeds from the sale of this book will go towards purchasing items that will
enrich the learning environment at Laxey School.

Published by the Friends of Laxey School - Caarjyn Scoill Laksaa
Registered Charity No. 809

First published 2008

ISBN 978-0-9560587-0-6

Design & Typesetting: Jane Ogden
Editor: Sue King
Project Co-ordinator: Allison Ratcliffe
Sponsorship Co-ordinator: Bernie Sullivan
Treasurer: Jane Clague

Printed by Mannin Media Group Ltd
Media House, Cronkbourne, Douglas, Isle of Man IM4 4SB
Telephone: 01624 696565 Fax: 01624 625623
Email: mail@manninmedia.co.im

COVER IMAGE: Laxey Harbour courtesy Barry Ogden

CONTENTS

SPONSORS 3-4

CHAPTER ONE   **Soups and Starters** 5

CHAPTER TWO   **Fish and Shellfish** 13

CHAPTER THREE   **Main Courses** 23

CHAPTER FOUR   **Vegetarian** 41

CHAPTER FIVE   **Desserts** 49

CHAPTER SIX   **Cakes, Bakes & Younger Makes** ..59

CHAPTER SEVEN   **Miscellaneous** 75

MANX GLOSSARY 84

INDEX   ....INSIDE BACK COVER

All recipes on the following pages refer to Manx produce where possible, but substitutions may sometimes be necessary.

Oven temperatures:	Gas	Fahrenheit	Celsius (as used in the book)
Slow	2	300	150
Moderate	4	350	180
Hot	6	400	200
Very hot	8	450	230

Weights

25 grams (g)	= 1 ounce (oz)
50g	= 2 oz
75g	= 3 oz
110g	= 4 oz
150g	= 5 oz
175g	= 6 oz
200g	= 7 oz
225g	= 8 oz (½ lb)
350g	= 12 oz
450g	= 16 oz (1 lb)

Liquid Volume

55 millilitres (ml)	= 2 fluid ounces (fl oz)
150ml	= 5 fl oz (¼ pint)
275ml	= ½ pint
425ml	= ¾ pint
570ml	= 1 pint
1.2 litres	= 2 pints
1.5 litres	= 2 ½ pints

1 Cup = 250ml or 9 fl oz

SPONSORS

SPONSORS

Devereau's Manx Kippers (Douglas & Peel)
The Island's largest kipper curers, smoking delicious, fully traceable, Manx kippers daily. Visit one of our shops for fresh local fish, lobster, crab & queenies.
www.isleofmankippers.com
Tel: 01624 673257 (Douglas) & Tel: 01624 843160 (Peel)

Greeba Farm Ltd - Mushrooms
Growing with care, NOT pesticides. Buttons to portobellos, our mushrooms are fresh and full of flavour. Available island-wide through Robinsons and Shoprite **and** direct from the farm.
www.greebafarm.co.im
Tel: 01624 851611

Island Seafare Ltd. Suppliers of fresh fish, smoked products, smoked salmon and shellfish. Our Manx scallops are famed for their size and quality and our fish is smoked according to an age old recipe. Mail order service available. **Contact Tim or Paddy Croft, Island Seafare, The Quay, Port St Mary** www.islandseafare.co.uk
Tel: 01624 834494

Laxey Village Commissioners
35 New Road, Laxey
Tel: 01624 861241 Fax: 01624 862623. www.laxey.org

Lonan Parish Commissioners
35 New Road, Laxey
Tel: 01624 861321

Mann Speciality Foods.
Producers of Ratcliffe's Manx Honey
Suppliers of speciality jams, chutneys and confectionery. Available from local shops and heritage sites throughout the Island.

Manx Organic Network (MON)
A voluntary organisation made up of consumers, growers, farmers, processors and retailers. The MON is dedicated to the increased production and promotion of locally produced Manx organic produce. For further details, list of producers and where you can buy please visit our website www.manxorganicnetwork.com

One Stop Shop, Station Road, Ballaugh Tel: 897222
Convenience Store & Post Office, Cafe, Farmers' Market and Farm Shop. Purveyors of: seasonal game, smoked meats, quality locally hand made pies, groceries, epicurean fine foods, Manx honey, organic Manx free range eggs and fruit & vegetables grown in Ballaugh to organic principles.

Reads Fine Foods, New Road, Laxey
For quality Manx meat; fresh, seasonal fish and shellfish; Manx cheeses and fresh local vegetables plus a variety of organic products.
Tel:01624 863343

Shoprite - the original Manx Fair Trade Supermarket.
Tel: 01624 683333
Douglas - Little Switzerland & Chester Street;
Onchan - The Village Walk;
Peel - Derby Road & Michael Street;
Ramsey - Bowring Road & St Pauls Square;
Castletown - Arbory Street;
Port Erin - Bridson Street and
SHOPRITE LIVING Marina Lane, Port Erin

THANKS TO ALL THESE MANX ORGANISATIONS FOR THEIR GENEROUS HELP IN PRODUCING THIS BOOK

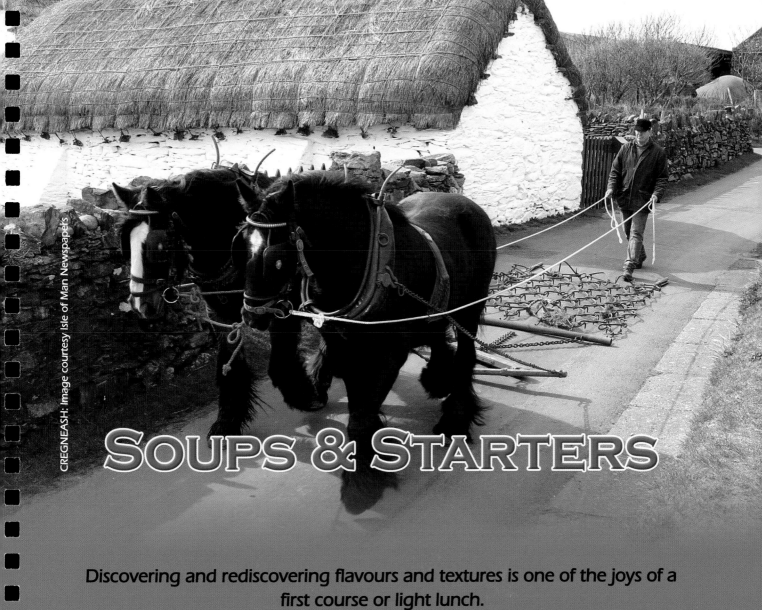

CREGNEASH: Image courtesy Isle of Man Newspapers

Soups & Starters

Discovering and rediscovering flavours and textures is one of the joys of a
first course or light lunch.
Fresh ingredients simply prepared are all that is required.
And, as many Islanders and visitors will testify, when you return to the
warmth and comfort of home after a day walking the hills and headlands
nothing quite hits the spot like a delicious bowl of homemade soup.

Creamy Pea Soup with Crispy Bacon

A perfect lunch dish for those with a smaller appetite - tasty, satisfying and nutritious. Or an easy to prepare first course for a dinner party. Take your pick!

25g Manx unsalted butter
1 large Manx onion, finely chopped
450ml vegetable or chicken stock
450g frozen peas (or fresh Manx peas, when in season)
Pinch of sugar
Salt and pepper
150ml Manx single cream
6 rashers smoked streaky Manx-cured bacon   Serves 4

Melt the butter in a large saucepan, add the onion and cook for 2-3 minutes until softened. Pour in the stock and bring to the boil. Add the peas, seasoning and sugar, bring back to the boil and simmer for about 3 minutes. Meanwhile, either grill the bacon under a very hot grill till crisp or pan fry in a hot pan, drain on kitchen paper then snip with kitchen scissors into small pieces. Set aside. When the soup is cooked allow it to cool slightly then blitz with a hand blender or in a liquidizer until smooth. Add the cream, stir gently and reheat (but do not allow to boil). Serve scattered with the crispy bacon and an extra swirl of lovely Manx cream!

"This lovely soup has great contrasting colours and textures. It's no wonder it's always so popular at Laxey's Lenten lunches - with people queuing for seconds and thirds!"

The Manning family

Stuffed Mushrooms

This dish makes a very impressive starter or an equally delicious light supper dish when teamed up with crusty bread and a salad.

8 large flat Manx mushrooms (Portobello are ideal)
6 - 8 Sun-dried tomatoes, drained and finely chopped
Handful of fresh chives, finely chopped
200g soft garlic and herb cheese
1 cup fresh wholemeal breadcrumbs
2 teaspoons dried Italian herbs (or 1 tablespoon fresh oregano, thyme and basil)
Extra-virgin olive oil

Image courtesy Isle of Man Newspapers

Serves 4   *Hedgehunter*

Preheat the oven to 200° C. Remove the stalks from the mushrooms and chop the stalks finely. Mix with the chopped sun-dried tomatoes, finely chopped chives and the cheese until well blended. Spread a large spoonful of the mixture in the centre of each mushroom then top with the breadcrumbs, Italian herbs and a drizzle of olive oil. Place on a baking tray and bake for 10-15 mins till golden brown.

This recipe is a great favourite amongst the office staff of Ballaseyr Stud in Andreas where the 2005 Grand National Winner Hedgehunter is now enjoying his retirement.

This recipe kindly donated by Trevor Hemmings - Owner of 2005 Grand National Winner 'Hedgehunter'

Pickled Herring

Herrings have played an important part in Manx food history for hundreds of years. Renowned for their versatility, they can be cooked fresh, smoked to produce kippers or cured in a solution of spiced pickle. This recipe is for the latter - a really good starter or light lunch dish.

4 fresh Manx herring, filleted into 8 fillets
60g salt
500ml water
500ml white wine vinegar or cider vinegar
1 teaspoon whole black peppercorns
2 - 3 teaspoons whole pickling spice
½ dried chilli (optional)
2 - 3 fresh bay leaves
1 large Manx onion, thinly sliced

To serve:
2 tablespoons sour cream mixed
with 2 tablespoons mayonnaise
Finely chopped parsley

Serves 4

Ask your fishmonger to fillet your fish into eight fillets. Pour the salt into a large non-metallic bowl, add the water and stir to dissolve. Immerse the herring fillets in the brine for 2 hours. Meanwhile, heat the vinegar, peppercorns, pickling spice, chilli (if using) and bay leaves until gently boiling, then allow to cool to room temperature. Remove the herring fillets from the brine, dry them on kitchen paper and pack them, alternating with the slices of onion, into a large, clean glass jar. Pour over the vinegar mix, ensuring the fish is properly covered. If you are a bit short add a bit more vinegar. Seal and place in the fridge for four days or more. To serve, remove the fillets and onions from the jar, drain them, top with a dollop or two of the sour cream mixture and sprinkle with chopped parsley. Serve with wholemeal rolls or rye bread.

"Try varying the pickle cure by adding sugar and using different spices such as juniper berries or allspice. And if you want to make 'rollmops' just wrap each fillet around a piece of pickled gherkin and secure with a cocktail stick before putting in the curing mixture."

The Taylor Family

Cream Of Carrot And Bacon Soup

This delicious soup with its carefully balanced flavours is a good way of getting lots of good Manx vegetables into your children if they're not that way inclined!

1 oz Manx butter
8 rashers rindless Manx-cured back bacon, diced
1 large Manx onion, peeled and finely chopped
1 lb fresh Manx carrots, peeled and finely chopped
2-3 sticks of Manx celery, finely chopped
¼ to ½ Manx turnip, peeled and finely chopped
1 tablespoon Manx plain flour
2 pints of chicken stock
Ground black pepper

Serves 4- 6

Image courtesy Allison Ratcliffe

The annual Southern Agricultural Show, held at Castletown

Heat the butter in a large pan and fry the chopped onion and bacon for about 5 minutes until starting to colour. Add the remaining vegetables and cook for a further five minutes until they begin to soften. Add the flour and cook, stirring, for a further minute. Gradually pour in the stock and bring to the boil. Season to taste and simmer for 30-40 minutes until the vegetables are soft. Cool slightly then puree in a blender. Return to the pan, re-heat, taste and adjust the seasoning.

(Salt can be added but you may find you don't need it as the bacon adds it naturally).

The Quayle family

Beetroot Soup

A traditional Polish recipe which makes the most of flavoursome fresh Manx root vegetables. Long slow cooking brings out the wonderful flavours and colours of the vegetables, which are removed after cooking to create a delicate pink soup.

2 chicken drumsticks or thighs, skinned
2½ pints water
2 Manx carrots
1 Manx parsnip
2 sticks Manx celery
1 Manx leek
1 small Manx onion
Salt and pepper
4-5 medium Manx beetroots, peeled and grated
100mls Manx single cream
Squeeze of fresh lemon juice   **Serves 4**

Place the chicken in a medium saucepan, add the water, bring to the boil and simmer for 15 minutes. Meanwhile, peel the carrots, parsnip and onions and chop into small chunks. Wash the leek and slice thinly, chop the celery and add all the vegetables to the pan. Season with salt and pepper and bring back to the boil, reduce to simmer and cook, covered, for a further 45 minutes. Remove the chicken from the pan using a slotted spoon then add the grated beetroot and continue to simmer for a further 30 minutes. Strain the stock, discarding the vegetables, add the lemon juice and cream and season to taste with salt and pepper..

The traditional Polish way to serve this soup is with a side dish of boiled potatoes sprinkled with fresh Dill.

"SMACZNEGO!!!" (Polish for 'Enjoy!')

Zosia Anscombe and family

Hearty Lentil Soup

A recipe that literally 'warms the cockles of your heart' - this fragrant, winter soup is the stuff that memories are made of.

1 Manx onion (finely diced)
1 piece of bacon or gammon (or you can use bacon bones or packet bacon)
6 Manx carrots, peeled (3 finely diced, 3 grated)
1 packet red lentils
2-3 pints of water
3-4 medium size Manx potatoes (cut into small chunks)

Serves 4

Image courtesy Sarah Henthorn
Welcome to Laxey

Soak the lentils in water for an hour then rinse thoroughly. Meanwhile, place the bacon or gammon in a large pan and cover with water. Bring to the boil. Once it's boiling skim any froth from the surface and add the onion, carrots, lentils and potatoes. There's no need for salt as the bacon is salty enough. Bring back to the boil, then turn the heat down and simmer gently for 1- 1½ hours. Stir often during cooking as the lentils can stick to the bottom of the pan. Remove the bacon, dice finely and return to the pan.

Serve at once with crusty bread or allow to cool and reheat the next day when it will taste even better.

"When I was a little girl attending Laxey School I used to run home every day for lunch, as did most of the children. I loved the cold winter days when I'd arrive home to find Mum in the kitchen and the smell of the lentil soup cooking. It was always my favourite. When I cook it now I always think of Mum."

Carolyn Scarffe - Laxey School Nursery Nurse

Traditional Manx Broth

This 'winter warmer' really is a family-sized quantity, best made the day before you plan to eat it. Then you can take the whole family for a bracing walk along the Raad Ny Foillan (Manx coastal path) and look forward to arriving home to a ready-cooked hearty dinner!

A brisket of Manx beef (1.5-2kg)
300g pearl barley
1 Manx Savoy cabbage
1 Manx swede
1 Manx carrot
1 Manx leek
1 large bunch of fresh parsley or 1 teaspoon dried parsley
5 litres of water
Salt and pepper

Serves 4 - 6

Place the brisket and barley in a large saucepan and cover with the water, bring to the boil and simmer for 1 hour. Skim off any scum that rises to the surface as it's cooking. Meanwhile, peel the vegetables and thinly slice them. Add to the pan, season well and simmer until cooked, about 20 minutes. Remove the meat, allow to cool slightly then cut or shred into small pieces. Return to the pan, check the seasoning and add the chopped parsley.

If eating straightaway, serve with crusty bread, but the broth will taste even better if eaten the following day when it becomes rich and thick.

The MacMillan family

FISH & SHELLFISH

The sea around our Island is home to basking sharks, whales, dolphins and seals. The rivers are home to wild salmon and trout.
Our locally caught fish and shellfish are delicious and plentiful - queen scallops, lobster and crab are available all year round and King scallops from November to May... and we mustn't forget the iconic Manx kipper!

Velvety Crab Soup

A beautiful, rich soup best made on a day when fresh crab has just been landed in Peel, Port St Mary, Laxey or Ramsey. Organic Manx vegetables are widely available from the Island's farmers' markets.

8 organic Manx tomatoes, halved
3 oz Manx butter
2 organic Manx carrots
2 organic Manx onions
2 organic Manx celery sticks
1 large organic Manx leek
1 garlic clove, finely chopped
2 fl.oz brandy
½ bottle white wine
½ teaspoon dried basil

½ teaspoon dried tarragon
1 lb fresh Manx Crab meat (mixed or all brown, but not all white)
3-4 pints vegetable stock
2 oz white rice, uncooked
A pinch cayenne
¼ pint Manx single cream
Juice of ½ lemon
Salt and pepper to taste
A splash of oil and butter

Serves 4

Heat your oven to 180°C. Place the tomatoes in a shallow oven-proof dish and cook in the oven for about 20 - 30 minutes until soft. Meanwhile, wash, peel and roughly chop the vegetables. Heat the oil and butter in a large soup pan, add the vegetables and garlic, cover the pan and cook for about 10 minutes until the vegetables are softened but not coloured. Turn up the heat, pour in the brandy and boil until the liquid has evaporated then add the wine and allow a little of that to evaporate. Next pour in about 3 pints of stock and add the herbs, crab meat and cooked tomatoes. Simmer gently for about 15 minutes. Add the uncooked rice and simmer again, covered, for about 30 minutes (don't worry about overcooking the rice). Allow to cool slightly then pour into a blender and whizz until smooth. If it's too thin, boil to reduce, if it's too thick, add more stock. Reheat and just before serving pour in the cream and lemon juice and season to taste.

The Watson family

Scallops Baked with Breadcrumbs

A quick and easy summer dish - this recipe takes great advantage of our proximity to the sea. King scallops are available between November and May.

Allow 2-3 large Manx scallops or 8-10 Manx queenies per person

12 large scallops, cleaned and cut into 4
(or approximately 40 queenies)
8 tablespoons white wine
4 tablespoons Manx butter, cut into small
cubes, plus extra for greasing
3 oz fresh white breadcrumbs
1 tablespoon lemon juice
1 tablespoon fresh parsley, finely chopped
plus extra for garnish
Salt and pepper

Serves 4

Image courtesy Chris Sharpe

Chris Sharpe

Pre-heat your oven to 180°C.
Butter an ovenproof dish and coat the bottom
and sides with a thick layer of breadcrumbs. Remove any black 'bits' from the scallops or queenies then place them in the dish sprinkled with the wine, lemon juice and chopped parsley. Season with salt and pepper and cover with the remaining breadcrumbs.

Dot the top thickly with butter and bake for approximately 40 minutes if using large scallops or 20 minutes if using queenies. Sprinkle with chopped parsley and serve while hot.

"I've always loved being out on the sea, either in my kayak or a friend's boat, and there's no better food than locally caught fish and seafood - enjoy it seasonally, support measures to ensure that it's harvested sustainably and celebrate the fact that eating it adds fewer greenhouse gases to the atmosphere than choosing foods from distant shores."

This recipe kindly donated by Chris Sharpe - Principal Editor, Manx Bird Atlas.

"The Hairy Bikers" Scallop Spring Rolls with Five-spice & Coriander

Crunchy textures, an exciting twist of Oriental 'heat' and the divine delicate flavour of fresh, local shellfish make this recipe a real winner. The clean waters around the Isle of Man are a wonderful natural environment for queenies and scallops, both of which are sensitively harvested to help maintain our precious seabeds. They only have short seasons though, so make the most of them while they're in the shops.

12 large Manx scallops cut into four pieces (or 24 Manx queenies, halved)
12 sheets spring roll pastry
A sprinkling of five spice powder
12 Coriander leaves
1 teaspoon corn flour mixed with 50 ml water to form a paste

<u>For the Dipping Sauce</u>
1 red chilli (seeded and chopped)
1 clove of garlic, crushed
Juice of half a lemon
1 tablespoon soy sauce
1 tablespoon dry sherry

<u>For the salad</u>
100g Mooli (a long white Japanese vegetable of the radish family available locally in specialist Oriental greengrocers)
30g chopped pickled ginger
4 spring onions, shredded
Groundnut oil for deep frying

Makes 12, Serves 4

Image courtesy Department of Tourism and Leisure

The Hairy Bikers

On a lightly floured board lay out a sheet of spring roll pastry. In the middle near one end lay a row of four scallop quarters, sprinkle with five spice powder and tear a coriander leaf equally over the scallops.

Using the cornflour and water paste, seal the spring roll pastry as you go and roll up into a spring roll. If it starts to get too thick, cut off the excess pastry. Make 12, set aside on an oiled plate and cover with damp kitchen roll to stop them drying out.

To make the salad, cut the mooli into strings and place on a plate with a heap of spring onions and pickled ginger.

Make the dipping sauce by combining the chilli, garlic, lemon juice, soy sauce and sherry. Put into a little pot on the plate.

Heat about 2½ inches of groundnut oil in a deep frying pan and when very hot cook the spring rolls until golden.

Remove onto kitchen towel to drain, then place on to the salad next to a portion of pickled ginger and spring onions. Dip the spring rolls into the sauce and add the mooli, onions and ginger as you like.

Recipe kindly donated by Dave Myers and Si King a.k.a 'The Hairy Bikers', enthusiastic food ambassadors for the Isle of Man (oh, and they're pretty keen on the TT as well!).

Salmon & Queenies, Laxey-Style!

A perfect dish to entertain friends 'al fresco' on a warm summer's evening - Laxey is, after all, named after the Viking's word for salmon and proximity to the sea is one of the many charms of this pretty harbourside village.

2 salmon fillets
8 oz Manx queenies
6 rashers of rindless Manx-cured bacon
1 Manx onion
2 glasses of dry white wine
5 fl oz Manx double cream
1 teaspoon chopped garlic
A knob of Manx butter

A splash of fresh lemon juice
Salt and pepper
2 tablespoons Manx cheddar cheese, grated

Serves 2 as a main course or 4 as a light lunch

Pre-heat the oven to 180°C. Place the salmon on a large sheet of foil. Top each piece with a knob of butter, flourish of garlic, splash of wine and lemon juice. Form the foil into a loose parcel and bake in the oven for 10 minutes. Meanwhile, check the wine is ok by careful sampling...

Heat a large frying pan and lightly saute the chopped onions and chopped bacon without allowing to brown. Increase the heat, add the queenies and toss together for about a minute. Pour in the remaining 1½ glasses of wine and simmer until slightly reduced. Remove from the heat and stir in the cream to thicken the sauce. Season to taste.

Remove the salmon from the parcels and place in a shallow oven proof dish, pouring any juices into the queenie sauce. Pour the queenies and sauce over the salmon and top with a sprinkling of cheese. Grill until golden brown.

Serve with seasonal Manx vegetables, new potatoes and salad, a wedge of lemon and, of course, a chilled glass of white wine!

The Henthorn family (and Richard in particular!)

Lobster, Mango & Coriander Omelette Rolls

A light summer evening meal, a mouth-watering starter or even a special Sunday brunch dish - this lovely recipe is definitely one to share with people who love good food simply prepared.

4 medium Manx free-range eggs
3 spring onions, finely sliced
1 teaspoon fish sauce
2 dessertspoons cold water
1 tablespoon peanut oil
250g fresh Manx lobster meat, cut into small pieces
1 ripe mango, peeled and sliced
Small handful of fresh coriander, lightly chopped

Serves 4

Image courtesy Sarah Henthorn
Niarbyl Bay

In a large bowl whisk the eggs lightly. Add the spring onions, fish sauce and water. Pour a dash of oil into a small frying pan and bring up to a moderate heat then pour in a quarter of the egg mixture and swirl it around to make a thin omelette. Cook for a minute or so until the top is beginning to set, then flip it over to cook the underneath for a few more seconds. Slide onto a plate and keep warm. Repeat three more times until you have four omelettes. To serve, place each omelette on a plate, divide the lobster meat and mango between them, sprinkle with coriander and roll up. For a complete main course dish, serve with a side salad.

"As a former professional deep sea diver the sea is never far from my thoughts and whenever possible I try to get out on my boat to catch some fresh Laxey Bay lobsters. This recipe, which originated in New Zealand, is perfect for our sweet, locally caught Lobster..."

Laxey Villager Glen Boyden

Trout & Bacon

Excellent freshwater fishing is one of the bonuses of the Island's bountiful reservoirs and clean, fast-flowing rivers.

6 Manx rainbow trout, filleted and skinned (12 fillets)
6 very thin slices of bacon (or parma ham)
1 teaspoon dried tarragon (or 1 tablespoon fresh)
2 tablespoons fresh lemon juice
1 small cup white wine

5 oz Manx double cream
2 tablespoons chopped Manx parsley

Serves 6

Pre-heat your oven to 190°C. Season the fillets with salt and pepper. Cut the bacon in half lengthways then stretch it with the back of a knife and place a piece over each fish fillet. Sprinkle with the lemon juice and tarragon. Roll up the fillets from the thick end to the thin and arrange them in an ovenproof dish. Pour the wine round the fish and bake about 15 minutes. Remove the fish to a serving dish and stir the cream and parsley into the wine. Serve the rolls with a little of the sauce spooned round, alongside some oven-roasted new potatoes and salad.

The Laxey Blacksmith (who loves his fishing rod almost as much as his anvil!)

Spicy Tiger Prawns

A delicious recipe for that 'special night in'! It also works well using queenies instead of prawns.

1 tablespoon Manx salted butter
12 - 16 shell-on raw Tiger prawns
1 fresh chilli, finely chopped, seeds removed

1 - 2 cloves garlic, finely chopped
1 glass dry white wine

Serves 2

Melt the butter in a large pan over a gentle heat, add the garlic and cook for a couple of minutes. Add the finely chopped chilli and cook for another minute. Turn up the heat, throw in the tiger prawns, add the white wine, give another stir then quickly put the lid on the pan. Leave until the prawns go a beautiful deep pink colour - only two minutes or so. The second they're all cooked through, transfer everything to a big dish and serve with crusty bread to mop up the garlicky juices, and chilled champagne.

Trish Dudley- Deputy Head Teacher, Laxey School

Kipper Paté

Well, what can we say about this - the kipper is to the Isle of Man what the haggis is to Scotland - a national treasure.

1 Packet of Manx kipper fillets
300-400g Manx butter
15-20ml Manx double cream
15ml fresh lemon juice
Pinch cayenne pepper
Pinch ground mace

To Serve
Lime marmalade
**Fresh Manx brown
  bread**

Glen Road, Laxey
Image courtesy Sarah Henthorn

Remove the kippers from the packet and stand them in a tall jug then cover them completely with boiling water. If necessary place a plate over the jug to keep the kippers under the water. Leave submerged for 5 minutes.

Remove from the water carefully, peel off the skin (it doesn't matter if a little is missed) then chop roughly into small pieces. Melt the butter then pour into a food processor with the chopped kippers and blend quickly until fairly smooth. Add the remaining ingredients and blend completely until very smooth. Pour into a serving bowl or individual ramekins. To achieve a 'professional' finish you can cover the surface with more melted butter. Refrigerate until set and serve with fresh bread and lime marmalade.

This is a great recipe for people who like the taste of kippers but don't like the fiddly bones. Also the kippers are 'jugged' to cook them so they won't leave you with a smelly ktichen! Surprisingly, the idea of serving kippers with lime marmalade works a treat... it's like having redcurrant jelly with meat paté.

Jean Aksoy - Head teacher, Laxey School

Olde Manks Sea Delight

So quick, so fresh - so Manx!

1 large Manx onion, finely chopped
1 tablespoon fresh parsley, finely chopped
1 clove garlic, finely chopped
1 lb fresh Manx queenies
6 oz large raw prawns
8 oz cod (or other local white fish) fillet (diced)
6 fl oz dry white wine
4 fl oz fish stock
Salt and black pepper
8 oz fresh Manx double cream
1 tablespoon brandy
1 teaspoon cornflour (optional)

Serves 2

Cook the onion in butter until soft and 'pearly'. Add the parsley and garlic then add the queenies, prawns, diced cod, wine, and fish stock together with seasoning and cook for 1 - 2 mins.

Add the cream and brandy and, if necessary, thicken with the cornflour mixed with a little cold water.

Bring back to simmer & cook for two more minutes.

This is best served with rice, lemon-buttered Manx new potatoes or even buttered bonnagh, and a crisp green salad.

Recipe kindly donated by Mike Quirk, Chef at the Creg-Ny-Baa restaurant, run by the Teece family of Laxey

Image courtesy Sarah Henthorn

MAIN COURSES

Farming is an integral part of Island life.
For many years Manx farmers have been quietly rearing fully traceable
animals to high welfare standards on small farms.
Animals, including specialist breeds such as Loaghtan lamb, Gloucester Old
Spot, Aberdeen Angus and continental cattle breeds, can be seen grazing
outdoors on lush green fields all year round...

Scrumptious Summer Chicken

Sitting by the side of the sparkling Laxey river on a warm summer's evening, friends gather to enjoy some good food, good wine and an unbeatable setting. What better dish to give them than this simple chicken recipe that can be prepared ahead up to the last stage and finished off just before serving.

4 boneless/skinless chicken breasts,
   pounded thin
Sea salt and freshly ground black pepper
2 large Manx free-range eggs
1 tablespoon Manx milk
60g plain Manx flour
200g dry breadcrumbs (made by whizzing
   day-old Manx white bread in food processor)
1 tablespoon olive oil
1 ball of fresh mozzarella cheese, sliced
50g grated Parmesan cheese

For the sauce
1 tablespoon olive oil
2 shallots, finely chopped
1 clove garlic, finely sliced
250g cherry tomatoes
½ teaspoon dried basil
Sea salt and freshly ground black
   pepper

Fresh basil to garnish   Serves 4

Preheat the oven to 200°C. Season the chicken fillets on both side with a little salt and pepper. Lightly beat the eggs together with the milk. Dust each chicken breast in flour, then dip in the beaten eggs and coat in the breadcrumbs. Sauté the chicken breasts in a little hot olive oil until golden brown - approximately 2 minutes on each side. Drain the cooked chicken on kitchen paper, then remove to a baking tray.

 To make the tomato sauce heat some oil in a heavy based pan. Add the shallots and garlic and cook for 2-3 minutes until softened. Add the tomatoes and basil. Allow the tomatoes to soften. Season to taste with salt and pepper. Spoon a little tomato sauce over each chicken fillet. Top with a round of mozzarella and sprinkle with the grated parmesan. (At this stage the dish can be covered and placed in the fridge to finish later). Bake in the oven for approximately 8 minutes, until the chicken is cooked and the cheese is melted and golden. Garnish each chicken breast with fresh basil and serve with sautéed or roasted mini potatoes and a green salad. Enjoy!

The Clegg Family

Quiche Annemarie

The deep, golden yellow colour of this rich, cheesey tart comes from eggs produced by happy, outdoor-reared Manx hens. Add to that some crisp, locally cured bacon and the very best in dairy produce and you have a nutritious treat for all the family.

For the Short crust pastry
8 oz Manx plain flour
4 oz Manx lightly salted butter,
  cut into small cubes
1 Manx free-range egg
2 tablespoons cold water

For the filling
1 teaspoon olive or vegetable oil
8 rashers Manx-cured streaky
  bacon, cut into small pieces

1 large Manx onion, chopped.
1 cup Manx mushrooms, sliced
6 oz Manx mature cheddar cheese, grated
6 large Manx free-range eggs
2 large cartons of Manx double cream
½ teaspoon salt and
½ teaspoon ground black pepper

Serves 8-10

To make the pastry, place the flour, butter, egg and water in a food processor and whizz for a minute or so until the mixture starts to bind together into a ball of dough. Remove from the processor, wrap in clingfilm and chill in the fridge for half an hour. Pre-heat your oven to 200°C and grease a 30cm flan tin. Remove the dough from the fridge, sprinkle flour onto a large working surface and roll the pastry out thinly into a circle large enough to line the base and sides of your flan tin. Prick the base of the pastry with a fork and cover with a sheet of greaseproof paper or baking parchment. Cover the paper with dried beans, ceramic baking beans or even tiny pebbles and bake the pastry blind for 10 minutes. Remove from the oven and take out the beans and paper. While the pastry is cooking heat the oil in a large frying pan and cook the bacon, onion and mushrooms until lightly browned. Allow to cool. Whisk the eggs and cream together in a large bowl and season. Add the bacon mix to the liquid then pour into the pastry case sprinkling half the cheese as you go. Cook in the oven for about 20 mins until the mixture starts to set then sprinkle the rest of the cheese over the top of the quiche. Cook for a further 20 minutes till well risen and golden brown.

The Sykes family

Perfectly Peppery Pot Roast

A firm family favourite which has the children eating all kinds of vegetables they don't realise are in it!

Image courtesy Barry Ogden

Ballaglass Glen

2 tablespoons suet or light olive oil
1 lb rolled rib or top rump of Manx beef
2 Manx carrots, peeled and chopped
1 Manx onion, chopped
1 Manx turnip, peeled and chopped
1 Manx leek, washed and chopped
8 small Manx mushrooms, cut into quarters
½ pint red wine
1 teaspoon dried Herbes de Provence (or 1 teaspoon each fresh chopped rosemary, bay, thyme)
½ dozen black peppercorns   Serves 4

Pre-heat your oven to 150°C. Melt the suet (or heat the oil) in a heavy frying pan over a low heat. Turn up to high and brown the meat all over - this will take about five minutes. Place in a large heavy-based casserole dish and sprinkle with the herbs and peppercorns. Pour the wine over the beef and place the chopped vegetables around the meat. Cover and place in the oven for 2 hours. Once cooked, remove the meat from the dish and carve into slices. Remove the vegetables with a slotted spoon and place in a bowl, puree with a hand blender, adding the meat stock to make a thick sauce. Pour the sauce over the meat, cover and keep warm while cooking new potatoes and peas to accompany the dish. Leaving the meat for a little while makes it even more moist and tasty.

Laxey Teacher Kelly Charman and family

Rich Manx Beef & Beer Casserole

Imagine a dark Manx winter's night when it's blowing a gale, the rain is horizontal - and you're cosy at home tucking into a big dish of this fantastic, aromatic stew. Another great recipe that tastes even better when made the day before it's eaten.

Olive oil
3-4 slices Manx bacon, cut into small pieces
2 Manx onions (peeled and sliced) or 12 button onions (peeled only)
2 lbs matured Manx stewing steak, cut into cubes
1 tablespoon Manx plain flour
3 Manx carrots, peeled and chopped
Salt and black pepper
1 heaped teaspoon Dijon mustard
1 level teaspoon granulated brown sugar
Handful mixed fresh thyme and parsley, finely chopped
10 oz Manx chestnut mushrooms, whole
1-2 pints vegetable stock
1 large bottle of Manx beer

<u>Topping</u>
Manx crusty bread, mustard and Manx mature cheddar (grated)

Serves 4

Pre-heat the oven to 150°C. Fry the bacon till slightly coloured, add the onions and cook till starting to brown. Remove from the pan. Raise the heat, add a bit more oil to the pan and fry the meat in small batches until evenly browned, removing each batch from the pan as you go. Place a large metal casserole dish (suitable for hob and oven use) on a low to medium heat on the hob. Transfer the bacon, onions and steak into the casserole and sprinkle the flour over the meat and vegetables, stirring well to coat. Slowly add the beer to the mixture, stirring as you go. As it comes to the boil it will thicken, so to get the required gravy consistency slowly add the stock (the sauce will get thinner as it cooks so don't add too much. You can always add more stock if necessary at the end of cooking time). Add the carrots, seasoning, mustard, sugar and herbs. Bring to the boil then cover and put in the oven for about 1½ hrs. Remove from the oven, taste the gravy and adjust the seasoning if necessary. Depending on the beer used you may need to add a little more sugar or mustard too. Stir well and add the mushrooms, cover with a layer of crusty bread "buttered' with mustard and sprinkled with Manx Mature Cheddar. Return to the oven, uncovered, for a further 15 minutes or until the cheese is melted and golden.

The Ratcliffe family

NIARBYL BAY - Image Courtesy of Richard Kinley www.richardkinley.co.uk

Lamb Tomato Bredy

Organic Manx lamb is a real treat, tender, sweet and full of flavour. If you're cooking for the family and want to use a slow-cooking cut try this dark and spicy lamb casserole. Ideal for cooking a day ahead as the flavour improves with time.

1kg Manx organic lamb, cut into large cubes
Seasoned flour
4 tablespoons olive or vegetable oil
6 bay leaves
1kg Manx onions, peeled and sliced
4 cloves garlic, finely chopped
1 teaspoon chilli powder (or less, according to taste)
2 cinnamon sticks, broken in two
1kg fresh Manx organic tomatoes, skinned and chopped
1 tablespoon tomato paste
60g dark muscovado sugar
Salt and pepper   Serves 4

Pre-heat your oven to 160°C. Dust the lamb in the seasoned flour, heat the oil in a large frying pan and brown the meat all over. Remove with a slotted spoon and set aside. Fry the onions with the bay leaves for a few minutes then turn down the heat and add the garlic, cinnamon sticks and chilli and cook for five minutes. Add the tomatoes, tomato paste, sugar and season to taste. Add the lamb and enough water to just cover the mixture. Stir well, bring to the boil then transfer to an ovenproof casserole dish with a well-fitting lid and place in the oven for three hours. Check the liquid levels halfway through cooking time and top up with more water if necessary. Serve with Manx organic mashed potatoes and organic savoy cabbage.

Miss Nadia Smith - Laxey School Teacher

Laxey School's Famous Cheese Pie

Okay, this dish may not be famous on the world stage - but it certainly is with the children - being the only recipe they constantly ask for! So, for all parents who have struggled to reproduce it at home, you can at last satisfy your children with the 'real thing'.

Mashed Manx potatoes (enough to feed your family)
Grated Manx cheddar cheese (approx 4-6 oz for 4 people)
Chopped tinned tomatoes (quantity according to taste)
Finely chopped onion

Pre-heat your oven to 180°C. Mix everything together. Put into an ovenproof dish and sprinkle with more grated cheese. Bake until piping hot and crusty on top.

Serve with salad or baked beans. Enjoy!

"The quantities are vague because not many people will be catering for between 60 and 110 children! - so you'll need to adapt it according to the size of your family"

Big thanks to the Laxey School Cooks Mrs Corlett and Mrs Renard for this much-loved recipe

Image courtesy Barry Ogden

Laxey School

Exotic Manx Lamb Pizza

A very unusual Middle-Eastern style pizza. The combination of ingredients may sound like unlikely but work together beautifully. Serve with a side dip of yoghurt, mint and cucumber.

1 large pizza base
4 tablespoons tomato pizza sauce or passata
400g Manx lamb mince
Pinch of salt and black pepper
¼ teaspoon ground nutmeg
¼ cup chopped fresh parsley
1 tablespoon chopped fresh mint
2 cloves garlic, peeled and finely chopped
1 small Manx onion, peeled and finely chopped
Juice of 1 lemon
¼ cup pinenuts
¼ cup raisins
2 Manx tomatoes, skinned, de-seeded and chopped

Serves 4

Preheat the oven to 225°C. Place the mince in a heavy-based saucepan, season with salt and pepper and cook on a medium heat, stirring occasionally, until evenly browned. Drain off any fat and add the nutmeg, parsley, mint, garlic, onion and lemon juice. Cook a further 4-5 minutes. Cool slightly. Spread the pizza base with the tomato sauce, then add the mince mixture. Top with pinenuts, raisins, and tomatoes and bake 15-20 mins or until golden brown.

The Ripton family

Jill's Coronation Chicken

The ultimate in adaptable recipes - you can add more or less of any of the flavourings to suit your taste, or change them completely - for instance, chopped dried apricots can be used instead of pickle.

Image courtesy Allison Ratcliffe

Lonan Millennium Monument

1 medium fresh chicken (Manx free-range if possible)
1 tablespoon vegetable oil
1 Manx onion, finely chopped
1 tablespoon curry powder
1 tablespoon tomato puree
1 glass red wine
juice of ½ lemon
1 tablespoon Branston pickle
10 fl oz mayonnaise
5 fl oz Manx double cream   Serves 4 - 6

Pre-heat the oven to 180°C. Lightly season the chicken and cook it in a covered roasting dish for approximately 1 hour and 20 minutes or until the juices run clear when pierced with a fork. Allow to cool completely. Remove the skin and bones and roughly break up the meat into small pieces. Gently fry the onion in the oil for a few minutes then add the curry powder, wine, tomato puree and lemon juice. Simmer the mixture gently until reduced and quite thick. Allow to cool then add the pickle, mayonnaise and cream.

Arrange the chicken on a serving plate and spoon over the sauce. Serve with rice, jacket potatoes, salads or as part of a buffet.

"This recipe is extremely easy to make and very forgiving if you get the measurements a little wrong. It can be made in advance if kept in the fridge and is great to take to parties."

Jill Bloom - Former teacher, Laxey School

Sticky Pineapple Meat Loaf

The smells from the kitchen while this is cooking will really get your appetite going! The pineapple gives the meatloaf a lovely rich tang and the sticky sweet 'n sour sauce and long, slow cooking make the meat meltingly tender.

For the meatloaf:
1lb Manx beef mince
¾ lb Manx pork sausage meat
¾ cup breadcrumbs (using day old Manx white bread)
¾ cup Manx full-fat milk
2 large Manx free-range eggs
2 tablespoons tomato ketchup
1 small tin pineapple rings (reserve the juice for the sauce)

For the sauce:
1 cup soft light brown sugar
2 tablespoons malt vinegar
¼ cup pineapple juice
1 teaspoon English mustard

Serves 4-6

Pre-heat your oven to 180°C. First make the meatloaf by mixing together the mince, sausagemeat, breadcrumbs, milk, eggs and ketchup. The mixture will be very wet. Take large spoonfuls of the mix and roll them into balls then flatten into patties. Place a layer of patties in a shallow rectangular dish then top with a layer of pineapple rings, then patties etc to form a long oblong shape. The top layer needs to be a meat layer. Cover with tin foil and cook in the oven for half an hour. Meanwhile, make the sauce by mixing together the brown sugar, vinegar, juice and mustard then remove the meatloaf from the oven, take off the tin foil and pour over the sauce. Place the foil loosely around the meat and return to the oven and cook for a further hour, basting every fifteen minutes. Remove the tin foil completely for the last fifteen minutes to allow the meat to brown. Serve in slices with mashed Manx potatoes and seasonal vegetables.

The Hanlon family

Mountaineer's Spaghetti Bolognese

Snaefell is the Isle of Man's only mountain, reaching a height of 621 metres above sea level. With views of England, Scotland, Ireland and Wales it makes a spectacular training ground for fell walkers, runners and, of course, mountaineers. This dish is ideal for anyone tackling Snaefell (or even more ambitious peaks!) as it includes pasta for slow-release energy and Manx beef and cheese for protein.

Image courtesy Mike Roberts Adventure Consultants
Phil pictured at Everest Base Camp

Image courtesy Isle of Man Newspapers
Phil Drowley

1 tablespoon olive oil
4 slices Manx-cured back bacon, chopped
1 large Manx onion, diced
1 lb Manx steak mince
½ teaspoon each of salt and freshly ground black pepper
1 clove garlic, peeled and finely diced
1 tablespoon fresh Manx parsley, finely chopped
1 tablespoon fresh oregano, finely chopped
1 tablespoon fresh basil, finely chopped
1 tin chopped tomatoes
2 tablespoons tomato paste
1 beef stock cube, dissolved in ½ cup boiling water
Small glass of red wine
2 heaped tablespoons Manx mature cheddar cheese, grated   Serves 4

In a large frying pan heat the oil and cook the bacon and onion till lightly brown. Add the mince, salt, pepper and garlic and stir well to break up the meat. Cook until it is thoroughly browned then drain off any fat. Add the tinned tomatoes, tomato paste, parsley and oregano, beef stock and red wine, stir well then bring to the boil. Lower the heat to a gentle simmer and cook, covered, for 45 minutes. When the sauce is almost ready cook some spaghetti in a large pan of rapidly boiling, salted water for ten minutes. Drain and transfer to a large serving dish, pour over the Bolognese sauce and chopped basil and mix in well till every strand of pasta is coated. Serve sprinkled with grated cheese.

Recipe kindly donated by Phil Drowley - Police Sergeant, IOM Constabulary and first Manxman to reach the summit of Mount Everest (at 5am on Saturday 24th May 2008.)

"I love this dish - my partner Lorraine makes a mean one and I tend to eat it after a good walk in the Island's hills . I did eat it at base camp on Everest and the camp cook, Chonggba Sherpa, wasn't half bad."

Coconut Curried Chicken

This wonderful, fragrant dish is Vietnamese in origin - indicated by its heady flavours of lemongrass, ginger, fish sauce and coconut.

1.5 kg chicken thighs, skinned and boned
1 large Manx onion
4 cloves garlic
2 x 10cm stems fresh lemongrass
25g piece fresh ginger, sliced
1 tablespoon mild curry powder
½ teaspoon ground turmeric
3 bay leaves
1 tablespoon peanut oil
1 large Manx potato, diced
400ml can coconut cream or milk
1 tablespoon fish sauce
2 medium Manx tomatoes, peeled and chopped
2 teaspoons chopped fresh coriander leaves   **Serves 4 - 6**

Cut the chicken thighs in half. Cut the onion into wedges and finely chop the garlic. Bruise the lemongrass by pressing it hard with the back of a knife. In a large bowl combine the chicken, garlic, onion, lemongrass, ginger, spices and bay leaves and mix well. Heat the peanut oil in a large pan and pour in the chicken mixture. Cook until the chicken is lightly browned all over. Add the diced potato, coconut cream or milk and fish sauce and simmer, covered, for about half an hour or until the chicken is tender. Discard the lemongrass and bay leaves, top with the tomatoes and coriander and serve immediately, accompanied by boiled rice and naan bread.

The Watt family

Pork Chops With Pear Sauce

The Isle of Man's heather-clad hills and rocky riverbeds are not only beautiful to look at - they also provide a superb training ground for the tough physical world of motorcycle enduro riding. This favourite recipe of Manx enduro champion David Knight has obviously fuelled him well, as he has won a number of world titles!

Image courtesy Isle of Man Newspapers

David Knight

3 pears, peeled, cored and finely chopped
3 tablespoons soft brown sugar
2 tablespoons lemon juice
¾ cup pear juice
2 tablespoons ground cinnamon
1 tablespoon vegetable oil
6 thin-cut boneless Manx pork chops   Serves 6

In a medium saucepan mix the pears, sugar, lemon juice, pear juice and cinnamon and bring to the boil. Simmer for 30 minutes, stirring occasionally until the sauce has thickened. Pour the sauce into a liquidiser and blend until smooth. Return to the saucepan, cover and simmer for 15 minutes over a low heat. Remove from the heat and allow to cool.

Heat the oil in a heavy frying pan over a medium heat and brown the pork chops, then cook for 4 minutes on each side. Transfer the chops to a serving dish and drizzle over the sauce. Serve with Manx carrots and creamy Manx mashed potatoes.

"This is my favourite recipe that my Grandma used to make me"

This recipe kindly donated by David Knight, World Enduro Champion 2005 and 2006; United States Grand National Cross-Country Champion 2007; World Indoor Enduro Champion 2007/08 and 2008 GNCC Champion.

Beans a la Clarkson

Some say this is too easy to be true, others say it has a magic all its own. All we know is - there's only one way to find out....

1 tin Heinz baked beans (only Heinz, no imitations allowed)
Lashings of Manx butter
6 drops of Tabasco
Good Manx white toast-sliced bread

Serves 1

Image courtesy Department of Tourism and Leisure

Jeremy Clarkson pictured with the Top Gear team

Find a can opener, open the tin of beans, put in a saucepan with two large knobs of butter and the Tabasco. Heat the beans slowly over a low heat for a long time, until the mixture becomes slightly mushy. The beans must still resemble the shape of a bean but the mixture must be mushy.

Place two slices of bread in the toaster and toast lightly. Butter the toast liberally making sure the butter reaches every corner. Place the beans all over the toast and serve immediately.

This recipe kindly donated by Jeremy Clarkson - Top Gear presenter, journalist, Manx resident and self-confessed non-cook. According to a source close to Jeremy he, in fact, is' not often seen in the kitchen. However, if left on his own the only recipe he does is (this) one."

Chicken Paprika

The cider and paprika give this dish a lovely golden colour and rich flavour.

3 large chicken breasts (Manx free-range if poss) skins removed
1 oz Manx plain flour
½ teaspoon salt
2oz unsalted Manx butter
2 tablespoons vegetable oil
1 large Manx onion, finely chopped
2 level teaspoons paprika
1 pint dry cider (reduced to ¾ pint by fast boiling in an open pan) or ¾ pint water
1 chicken stock cube
salt and pepper
¼ pint carton soured cream or crème fraiche
8 oz seedless white grapes, halved   Serves 3 - 4

Sprinkle the flour onto a plate and season with the salt and pepper. Cut the chicken into long strips and coat in the flour. Heat the oil and butter in a large frying pan and quickly saute the chicken, a few pieces at a time, until lightly brown. Remove from the pan with a slotted spoon. Add the onions to the pan and sauté until soft but not brown. Stir in the paprika and cook for one minute.

Add the cider or water and the crumbled stock cube. Bring to the boil and adjust seasoning. Add the chicken, lower the heat and simmer uncovered for about 30 minutes, stirring occasionally. Just before serving, stir in the soured cream and the halved grapes. Serve with rice and sweetcorn, green beans or broccoli. Delicious!

Mrs Blain
ICT Co-Ordinator - Laxey School

Cav's Baked Chicken Pasta

Manxman Mark Cavendish is one of the hottest competitors on the international cycling circuit - in 2008 he became the first British cyclist to win four stages of the Tour de France in one year. Fuelling his body for intensive training and competition requires a strict eating regime, but when he's at home this is what Mark really likes to eat!...

Mark Cavendish

500g fusilli pasta, cooked
1 smoked sausage, cut into chunky slices
2 chicken breasts, cooked and cut into bite-sized pieces
1 cup frozen peas and sweetcorn, mixed

<u>For the sauce:</u>
1 can condensed tomato soup
1 cup Manx full-cream milk
Six Manx tomatoes, peeled and chopped (or one tin chopped tomatoes)
Salt and pepper
Handful of fresh Manx-grown herbs (basil, thyme, mint), finely chopped
1 cup Manx mature cheddar cheese, grated

Pre-heat your oven to 150°C. Assemble the first four ingredients in an ovenproof dish, mix the sauce ingredients together (except the cheese) then pour over the pasta mix and sprinkle with grated cheese. Bake in the oven for 30 minutes or until nicely browned on top.

This recipe kindly donated by Mark Cavendish - reigning Commonwealth Games Points Race Champion; double World Madison Champion; double 2008 Giro d'Italia stage winner; four-times stage winner of the 2008 Tour de France and member of the British 2008 Olympic Cycling Team.

Almond Chicken

The almonds give both a delicate nutty flavor and creamy texture to this special dish. It's surprisingly easy and quick to prepare though and makes great use of fresh Manx chicken.

100g ground almonds
4 Manx free-range chicken breasts, boned and skinned
30ml corn oil
1 tablespoon Manx butter
1 small Manx onion, finely chopped
1 fresh chilli (optional), roasted, seeded and finely chopped
1 large Manx tomato, skinned, seeded and chopped
1 clove garlic, crushed
120ml chicken stock
1 pinch of salt
120ml Manx double cream
1 Manx tomato, cut into wedges
1 sprig fresh coriander

Serves 4

Pour the ground almonds onto a large plate and press the chicken onto them to give a light coating. Place the chicken on a separate plate and reserve the remaining almonds. Heat the butter and half the oil in a large frying pan and add the chicken, cooking for about 6 minutes until light brown on both sides. Remove from the pan and set aside. Add the remaining oil to the pan with the onion, chilli (if using), chopped tomato and garlic and fry gently for about one minute. Add the stock, salt and remaining ground almonds and bring to the boil. Return the chicken to the pan and reduce to a low heat. Cover and simmer for 20 minutes until cooked. Remove the chicken with a slotted spoon and transfer to a warmed serving dish then add the cream to the mixture in the pan, bring back to the boil and cook, stirring, until the sauce is thickened. Pour it over the chicken, garnish with the tomato wedges and coriander and serve with boiled rice.

Mrs Ana Rodan

Isle of Man Southern District Agricultural Society
Annual Summer Show
held at GREAT MEADOW - CASTLETOWN
Class 671 Exhibit No.
SECOND PRIZE
G. Sloan.
Mrs J.

VEGETARIAN

Image courtesy Allison Ratcliffe

Manx farmers are able to grow a wonderful variety of root, green and salad vegetables. Together with the experienced growers of the Manx Organic network they provide a plentiful supply of quality produce which in Spring even includes fresh local asparagus.
We also have our own mushroom farm, which is able to supply us with even the most exotic varieties.

Chestnut And Leek Pie

A lovely autumn dish to celebrate the end of the harvest, a time known in the Isle of Man as the mhelliah. Nowadays this is marked by many villages around the island holding charity auctions of fruit and vegetables. If you prefer to use fresh chestnuts they're freely available in the island's glens and woodlands during September and October. Just prick and boil them to remove the skins.

3 tablespoons sunflower oil
1 clove garlic, crushed
8 oz Manx shallots or small onions, peeled
10 oz small Manx button mushrooms
12 oz Manx leeks, washed and sliced
    diagonally
2 medium Manx parsnips, peeled and
    cubed
1 tablespoon tomato puree
2 tablespoons plain Manx flour

5 fl oz red wine
¾ pt vegetable stock
1 bay leaf
425g tin of whole peeled chestnuts
3 tablespoons chopped fresh parsley
Salt and ground black pepper
12 oz ready made puff pastry
1 Manx free-range egg, beaten

Serves 4

Pre-heat your oven to 200°C. In a large frying pan heat the oil and gently fry the garlic and shallots for 5 minutes. Add the remaining vegetables and tomato puree and cook for further 5 minutes. Sprinkle in the flour then gradually stir in the wine and stock. Add the bay leaf and chestnuts, cover and simmer for 10 minutes then stir in the parsley and seasoning. Using a slotted spoon, spoon the vegetables into a large ovenproof dish and pour over 10 fl.oz of the gravy mixture (put the remainder to one side).
Roll out three quarters of the pastry to fit the top of the dish and use the remaining pastry to roll out a strip to fit the edge of the dish. Place the strip around the dampened rim of the dish. Dampen the strip and place the lid on the top of the pie. Crimp the edges of the pie lightly to seal it then trim off any excess pastry and use it to decorate the pie. Cut a small slit in the centre to allow steam to escape. Finally brush the top of the pie with the beaten egg to glaze it. Bake in the oven for 35-40mins and serve with the remaining wine-flavoured gravy, accompanied by new or mashed potatoes.

The Callister family

Summer Vegetarian Terrine

Light and tasty, this terrine would make a lovely centre piece to a summer buffet.

1 tablespoon vegetable oil
1 Manx onion, peeled and finely chopped
2 sticks Manx celery, finely chopped
3 oz peanuts, finely chopped
2 oz ground almonds
1 teaspoon fresh marjoram (or ½ teaspoon dried)
1 teaspoon fresh thyme (or ½ teaspoon dried)
Salt and pepper to taste
6 firm Manx tomatoes, finely chopped

<u>Topping</u>
2 oz grated Manx mature cheddar cheese
3 oz fresh Manx brown breadcrumbs
1 tablespoon olive or vegetable oil
Serves 2

Image courtesy Barry Ogden
Port Erin

Heat the oven to 180°C. In a large frying pan heat the oil and sauté the onion and celery until soft. Add the nuts and herbs, season and mix well. Line the base of a deep oven proof dish or loaf tin with a layer of the celery mixture then cover with a thin layer of chopped tomatoes. Repeat till all the ingredients are used, pressing down firmly as you go.

To make the topping, mix together the cheese, breadcrumbs and oil then sprinkle over the vegetable mix. Bake in the pre-heated oven for about one hour and serve either hot or cold.

The Nettle family

Asparagus Tart

Fresh Manx asparagus is grown in the north of the Island and enjoys a short but bountiful season in early summer. Asparagus is always at its best when cooked shortly after picking and this is where locally grown really comes into its own. This delicate tart can also be made as individual tartlets for a dinner party starter or even as small canapés.

Large pre-baked shortcrust pastry case
4 medium Manx onions, peeled and finely chopped
50g Manx lightly salted butter
4 tablespoons Manx double cream
2 teaspoons white caster sugar
½ teaspoon salt
20 Manx asparagus tips (about 2-3 inches long)
2 tablespoons toasted pinenuts

Serves 4-6

In a large frying pan heat the butter and cook the onions, covered, over a very low heat until very soft. This will take about 20 minutes. Pour in the cream and cook, stirring, until it starts to thicken, then add the sugar and mix well. Allow to cool slightly then spoon the mixture evenly into the pre-cooked pastry case and keep warm in a low oven. Bring a large pan of water to the boil, add half a teaspoon of salt then blanch the asparagus for about three minutes or till tender. Drain but keep in the pan. Add a small knob of butter and quickly stir to coat the asparagus. Remove the tart from the oven, arrange the asparagus over the onion mixture then sprinkle with the toasted pinenuts and serve in slices straightaway.

Laxey Sketch Club (meet every Wednesday evening at Laxey Sailing Club)

Tynwald Baked Potatoes

A politician's life is all about multi-tasking and this favourite recipe from the Speaker of the House of Keys, Steve Rodan, shows just how easy it can be to turn a humble spud into a tasty dish - while grilling meat on the barbecue at the same time (which, Steve admits, is the only time he cooks!). He also recommends it as a meal on its own, topped with Parmesan cheese, tomatoes and parsley (and crispy bacon for meat eaters).

Steve Rodan

1 large Manx baking potato
1 Manx onion, peeled and sliced into rings
Large knob of Manx butter
1 clove garlic, finely chopped
Salt, celery salt and pepper

Serves 1-2

Make deep slits in the potato at ½ inch intervals taking care not to cut all the way through. Place onion slices, seasonings and butter in the slits. Top with sliced mushrooms.

Wrap well in two layers of baking foil.

Grill over hot, direct heat for 50 to 60 minutes on the barbecue - or if preferred, the potato can be baked in a hot oven at 200°C.

This recipe kindly donated by Steve Rodan, Speaker of the House of Keys

Mushroom Parcels

Wild field mushrooms are one of the bonuses of a walk in the green Manx countryside on an Autumn morning. Keep a basket handy just in case you spot the tell-tale white caps amongst the grass. But if you just want to enjoy the fresh air, cultivated Manx mushrooms give you just as much flavour (and you won't get your shoes wet!)

Filling
1 clove of garlic, chopped
8-10 oz Manx mushrooms (assorted) - chopped, sliced and ripped to give various textures
1 tablespoon Manx butter
Splash of olive oil
½ Manx onion, finely chopped
1 packet of dried mushrooms
2 tablespoons of Brandy
Fresh thyme
2 tablespoons Manx double cream (or more depending on the consistency of the finished mix)
Salt and pepper

To make the parcels
One packet filo pastry
Butter or vegetable oil
or
One packet of puff pastry

Cover the dried mushrooms with boiling water and leave to soak. While they are soaking, heat the butter and oil and fry the onions until soft then add the garlic and fresh mushrooms. Add some salt and a little thyme. Let the mushrooms really cook until any excess water has evaporated. Add the dried mushrooms and their soaking liquor to the other mushrooms and allow to cook until they are dry again. Add the brandy and once again cook off any excess liquid. Remove from the heat and add just enough cream to coat the mushrooms and make a bit of sauce. Allow to cool.

Use this filling and the filo pastry to make little, spring roll-style or samosa-shaped parcels or fill small squares of the puff pastry to make tartlets.

The Sullivan family

Sweet Potato & Vegetarian Sausage Hotpot

A flavoursome one-pot meal that can be adapted for meat-eaters simply by substituting Manx pork sausages for the vegetarian ones.

1 large sweet potato
½ butternut squash
Salt and black pepper
I large Manx onion
2 tablespoons vegetable oil
1 tin baked beans or haricot beans
6 large Manx tomatoes
3 tablespoons fresh Manx herbs (finely chopped fresh parsley, thyme and rosemary) or 3 teaspoons dried mixed herbs
½ teaspoon chilli powder (optional)
1 tablespoon tomato paste
1 cup vegetable stock
6 vegetarian sausages

Serves 4-6

Image courtesy Philip Clark

Snaefell Mountain Railway

Pre-heat your oven to 190°C. Peel the sweet potato and butternut squash, chop into one -inch chunks and place on a baking tray. Drizzle with one tablespoon of the oil, season with salt and pepper then bake for 30 minutes or until soft and slightly caramelized. While the vegetables are roasting, peel and finely chop the onion, heat the remaining oil in a large saucepan and sauté the onion until soft and just beginning to colour. Dip the tomatoes quickly in boiling water to soften the skin, cool slightly then peel and chop finely and add to the onions with the herbs, tomato paste and vegetable stock (and chilli, if using). Add the beans and simmer for fifteen minutes. While the bean mix is cooking, fry the sausages in a little oil until browned all over. Cut into chunks and add to the hotpot with the roasted squash and sweet potato. Simmer gently for a further five minutes then serve with crusty bread.

The Hanlon family

Parish Walk Cheese Muffins

The annual Parish Walk takes place on 85 miles of Manx roads and these more-ish, tasty muffins have helped boost the energy levels of many an athlete in training. They freeze well, so make plenty and they'll keep you going for miles!

1 cup Manx semi-skimmed milk
3 tablespoons melted Manx butter
1 large free-range Manx egg
1 cup mature Manx cheddar cheese, grated
½ teaspoon salt
1 tablespoon baking powder
2 cups Manx plain wholemeal flour

Makes 12 muffins

Lightly oil a 12-hole muffin tin and preheat the oven to 200°C.

Put the first 3 ingredients into a bowl and mix well, then add the remaining ingredients and blend until just mixed. Two-thirds fill the muffin tins and sprinkle a little extra grated cheese over the top of each muffin.

Bake for 15-20 mins or until the muffins are golden brown and spring back when touched.

"These muffins are quick and easy to make and make a lovely accompaniment to a bowl of soup or ploughman's lunch. If you're making them to take on a picnic, allow at least two per person as the first one just makes you want more!"

The King family

DESSERTS

Scene arranged by Braddan WI for Southern Agricultural Show 2008: Image courtesy Allison Ratcliffe

Picking your own fruit is not a new idea but it's still fun whether on a farm or
on the open moorland in search of wild bilberries and blackberries.
Fresh raspberries and strawberries bring a taste of summer.
Locally grown rhubarb, apples and plums make wonderful winter crumbles.
Of course, then all you need is a dollop of fresh Manx cream.

Rhubarb Fool Brulée

Rhubarb grows abundantly in the Isle of Man and is a staple of our very popular Farmer's Markets. The rhubarb season is only short however, so make the most of it with this soft, sweet and lovely-to-look at dessert.

1 lb fresh Manx rhubarb, washed, trimmed and cut into 3cm pieces
50g caster sugar
250g tub of mascarpone cheese
300g tub crème fraiche
3 tablespoons Grand Marnier or lemon juice
Grated zest of half an orange
125g Amaretti biscuits
3-4 tablespoons demerara sugar   **Serves 4**

Place the rhubarb in a large saucepan with the caster sugar and cook, covered, on a very gentle heat for 8-10 minutes, shaking the pan occasionally to prevent sticking. Allow to cool. Break the biscuits but don't crush them and set aside. In a large bowl mix the mascarpone, crème fraiche, liqueur (or lemon juice if preferred) and zest together until smooth and thick. Take an ovenproof soufflé or casserole dish and layer half the rhubarb, biscuits and cream then repeat with the rest. Place in the fridge until chilled. Two hours before serving remove from the fridge, sprinkle the demerara sugar over the cream and either chill (in which case the topping will go melted and fudgy) or caramelize under the hottest grill possible. Serve immediately as it will only stay crisp for a short time.

Cooked rhubarb freezes beautifully, so there's always plenty for winter crumbles - or you can puree it and add to champagne for a pink summer sparkler!

Fiona Shimmin - Bock Yuan Fannee, Manx Folk Dance Group

Kevin Woodford's Melting Chocolate Pudding

An after-theatre or concert supper would be the perfect setting for this luscious dessert. Invite friends round after a night at the Outdoor Shakespeare or Laxey Blues Festival and finish the evening with something special.

5 medium Manx free-range eggs
5 extra egg yolks
125g unrefined caster sugar
250g unsalted Manx butter
250g good quality dark chocolate (70% cocoa solids)
50g plain Manx flour, sieved

Serves 6 - 8

Image courtesy Kevin Woodford

Kevin Woodford

Whisk together the eggs, egg yolks and sugar until the mixture becomes light and fluffy and quite pale. Melt the chocolate and butter together in a bowl over a pan of hot water. Once melted, slowly add to the egg mixture until smooth. Add the sieved flour and fold through. Pour the mixture into buttered individual moulds and leave to chill in a refrigerator overnight. Cook in a preheated oven set at 180°C for about 10 to 15 minutes.

It's important not to overcook this pudding as the purpose is for the centre to remain as a liquid. The pudding is cooked once the top becomes firm and rises slightly.

This recipe kindly donated by Kevin Woodford - Manx resident, celebrity chef, food writer and television personality.

Rhubarb And Orange Crumble Cake

This is more of a dessert than a cake and makes a lovely finish to a Sunday lunch.

4 oz Manx butter
4 oz caster sugar
4 oz Manx self-raising flour
2 Manx free-range eggs
Finely grated rind of 1 orange
4 sticks of Manx rhubarb, chopped, sweetened and cooked till soft (or 2 cans of drained rhubarb)

For the crumble topping:
2 oz Manx butter
4 oz Manx plain flour
2 tablespoons granulated sugar
½ teaspoon ground cinnamon
Icing sugar for dusting

Pre-heat your oven to 190°C. Grease a 9 inch spring-release cake tin and line with greaseproof paper. To make the cake beat the butter, caster sugar, flour, egg and orange rind together in a bowl until well mixed and smooth. Spoon the mixture into the tin and spoon the rhubarb over the cake mixture. To make the crumble topping, sieve the flour into a large bowl and rub in the butter then stir in the granulated sugar and cinnamon. Sprinkle the crumble mixture over the rhubarb. Bake for 45-55 minutes or until firm to the touch and golden brown.

Dredge in icing sugar and serve warm, with Manx single cream.

The Quayle family

Indulgence

A wicked, yet wickedly simple recipe from Manx multi-media personality Alex Brindley - but the editor would like to apologise to Alex for renaming his dessert. Well, do you think 'splodge' (his choice) really does this creamy creation justice? It's gorgeous!

2 large pots of Manx double cream (284ml)
450g chocolate chip cookies
2 glasses of rosé wine

Image courtesy Alex Brindley

Alex Brindley

Pour the cream into a large bowl and whip until it is firm and forms soft peaks. Take one cookie and dunk it briefly in the wine. Take care not to actually soak it or it will fall apart. Using a palette knife, apply a generous amount of cream to one side of the cookie and place it, cream side inwards, against the edge of a large shallow dish.

Repeat the process with all the cookies, cream and wine until the entire dish is fully lined then fill in the centre in the same way.

Cover and refrigerate for at least an hour before serving.

"This is a University dessert...it's cheap, looks great, is terribly easy to make and very bad for you, but tastes amazing! (I eat far too much of it!)"

Recipe kindly donated by Alex Brindley - Manx Radio Breakfast Show Presenter, Film-maker, Writer, Director and Actor

Laxey Meringue Mess

A simple dessert that you can prepare in advance and let your guests put together themselves.

For the meringue
3 large Manx eggs
6 oz caster sugar

For the lime syrup
4 oz caster sugar
4 fl oz water
Zest of one lime, finely grated
4 fl oz fresh lime juice (approx. 3 limes)
1 level teaspoon arrowroot powder

For the cream cheese mixture
1 jar good quality lemon curd (see recipe on page 81)
200g cream cheese
200g plain fromage frais
1 tablespoon caster sugar
½ teaspoon vanilla extract

Serves 6-8

Firstly make the meringues. Pre-heat the oven to 130°C. Place a sheet of greaseproof paper on a baking tray. Whisk the egg whites in a clean bowl until they reach the 'soft peak' stage. Add the sugar a tablespoon at a time whisking well between each addition. Spoon the mixture in dessertspoonfuls onto the lined baking tray. Place in the oven and bake for 1-1½ hours then turn the oven off and open the door slightly to allow the meringues to dry out whilst letting the steam escape.

To make the lime syrup, place the sugar and water in a small, heavy based saucepan, bring slowly to a simmer then stir to dissolve the sugar. Add the lime zest and simmer very gently for 15 mins without reducing the volume. Meanwhile, mix the arrowroot with the lime juice in a cup and when the syrup is ready, pour it in, stirring all the time. Continue to heat gently and slowly return to simmering point until clear and slightly thickened. Remove from the heat and leave to go cold in the fridge.

In a bowl mix together the lemon curd, cream cheese, fromage frais, sugar and vanilla extract.

To serve, allow your guests to make their own desserts, layering meringues, lemon cheese and cream cheese mixture, topped with a splash of lime syrup.

The Ratcliffe Family

Chocolate Orange Torte

A decadent, but surprisingly easy, dessert which can be made up to a day ahead.

Image courtesy Allison Ratcliffe
Tynwald Day

5 Digestive biscuits, very finely crushed
2 x 284ml pots of Manx double cream
400g dark chocolate (50% solids is best)
3 tablespoons glucose syrup
Finely grated rind of 1 orange and 3 Tablespoons of juice
2 tablespoons of Orange liqueur (optional, or add 2 more tablespoons of orange juice)

Serves 10-12 people

Line a 9-inch round loose bottom or springform cake tin with cling film, placing a circle of greaseproof paper on the base. Sprinkle the finely crushed biscuits all over the base.

Place the chocolate, liquid glucose, orange rind, juice and liqueur in a microwave proof bowl. Microwave gently in 30 second bursts until the chocolate is melted. Stir the mixture until it is smooth.

In a separate bowl beat the cream until it begins to thicken. With a bendy spatula mix the cream into the chocolate mixture until it is thoroughly blended.

Pour the chocolate mixture carefully over the biscuit base. Cover with clingfilm and place in the fridge overnight. When set place a serving plate on top of the tin and turn the tin over, turning the biscuit base into a biscuit top.

Serve with fresh Manx raspberries or Manx strawberries and single cream.

This is such a rich dessert, but so very simple to make. Perfect for pudding on Christmas day as it's the only day when nobody worries about the calories!

The Kniveton Family

Minorca Christmas Pudding

No matter how much you eat on Christmas Day it's always best to leave room for a bit of Christmas pud - especially when it's as delicious as this one! Most of the work is in the steaming but if you make it up to three months in advance to allow the flavours to mature, it only needs reheating when the 'big day' arrives.

50g 2-day old white Manx bread
1 medium Manx free-range egg, beaten
50g Manx self-raising flour
1 level teaspoon mixed spice
225g mincemeat
1 tablespoon Manx full-fat milk
1 level tablespoon treacle

Serves 6

Place the bread in a food processor and whizz for 20 -30 seconds to make fine breadcrumbs. Pour into a large mixing bowl and add the beaten egg, sieved flour and spice. Add the mincemeat, milk and treacle and mix well together until thoroughly combined. Spoon into a large pudding basin (or six individual ones), cover with greaseproof paper then a double layer of tin foil, folding a crease in the middle to allow for expansion. Tie with string and place in a large saucepan half filled with simmering water. Cover tightly and simmer for four hours (two hours for small puddings). Check the water levels occasionally and top up with boiling water if necessary. At the end of cooking time, remove from the pan and set aside to cool thoroughly. When cold, turn out and wrap in greaseproof paper and a few layers of tin foil and store in an airtight container until Christmas Day. To reheat, unwrap the pudding and either steam again for half an hour or place, lightly covered, in the microwave and heat for 5 minutes or until hot right through.

"This never-fail pudding is a tradition in our house - the children love it - but we've also made small, individual versions to sell at Christmas Fairs and they've been really popular, with lots of people asking for the recipe - so, here it is!"

The Callister-Grant family

Sticky Toffee Pudding

Rich, sticky, simply oozing with temptation, this is a serious pudding that deserves total silence while it is eaten. Which should be done slowly and with great reverence...

3 oz Manx butter
5 oz caster sugar
2 large Manx free-range eggs
6 oz Manx self-raising flour
6 oz chopped dates
6 fl.oz boiling water
½ teaspoon vanilla extract
2 teaspoons 'Camp coffee' (or 1 teaspoon
   instant coffee dissolved in 1 tablespoon
   boiling water)
¾ teaspoon bicarbonate of soda

For the topping:
3 oz soft brown sugar
2 oz Manx butter
3 tablespoons fresh Manx double cream

Image courtesy Barry Ogden

Laxey Flour Mill

Serves 4 - 6

Preheat the oven to 150°C. Pour the boiling water over the dates. Add the coffee, bicarb of soda and vanilla extract and leave to stand. In a large bowl beat the sugar and butter till light and fluffy then beat in the eggs, one by one, then sift in the flour and finally add the date mixture. Pour into a lined 12" x 6" x 1" baking tray and cook for 45 minutes until firm and browned on top. Meanwhile, gently melt the topping ingredients together then prick the pudding all over its surface and pour the topping over to soak through. Allow to cool slightly in the tin before serving with more double cream or a scoop of Manx vanilla ice-cream.

The Henthorn family

Lemon Pudding

4 oz Manx butter, softened
6 oz caster sugar
Grated zest and juice of 3 large lemons
2 large Manx free-range eggs, separated
2 oz Manx plain flour
¾ pint Manx milk

Pre-heat your oven to 180°C. In a large bowl, beat the butter, sugar and lemon zest until fluffy. Add the two egg yolks then the lemon juice, flour and milk and mix well. (It may curdle slightly at this stage but don't panic).

In another large bowl whisk the egg whites until stiff and fold gently into the flour mixture. Spoon the mixture into an ovenproof dish then place the dish in a large tray half filled with water.

Bake for approximately one hour.

The Moffat family

Image courtesy Sarah Henthorn

The Sound

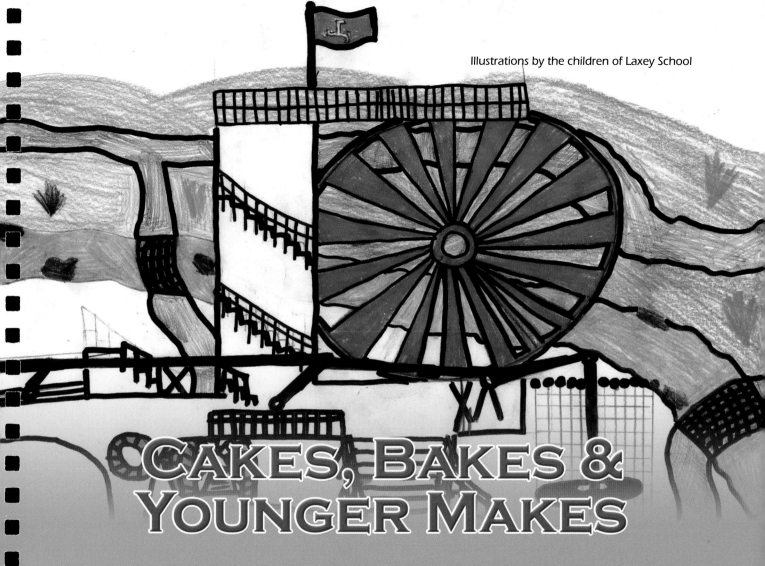

Illustrations by the children of Laxey School

CAKES, BAKES & YOUNGER MAKES

The secret of great baking is the ingredients. The Laxey Flour Mill is able to trace every bag of flour right back to the Manx farm on which the wheat was grown. The Isle of Man Creamery collects milk from local farms to produce fresh butter, buttermilk and cream. Our free ranging chickens provide the other essential...
And of course, the younger you can start learning to cook, the better.
At Laxey School children can grow their own food in their garden and greenhouse and then cook and taste their produce in the classroom.

Lemon Drizzle Cake

Mmmm, light and tangy - one slice of this delicious cake is never enough!

150g Manx butter, softened
150g caster sugar
2 Manx free-range eggs, beaten
Juice and grated zest of 1 lemon
150g Manx self-raising flour
4 tablespoons Manx milk
2 tablespoons icing sugar

Laxey Tram Station

Preheat the oven to 180°C. Beat the butter with caster sugar till creamy then gradually add the beaten eggs. Beat in the lemon zest and then add the sifted flour. Add the milk. The mixture should be of dropping consistency. Spoon the mixture into a 900g non-stick loaf tin and spread the surface flat with a spatula. Bake for 40 minutes then remove from the oven and leave in the tin.

Mix the icing sugar with the lemon juice, prick the top of the cake with a fork and pour the juice over while still warm.

Leave to cool for 15 mins then turn out onto a wire rack and allow to cool completely.

Hannah Newton - Laxey School teacher

Wheaten Marmalade Cake

This is quite a dense cake with a surprise twist of tangy bitter orange. Home-made marmalade is one of the great staples of the Manx parish fairs that abound in June and July. Head for your nearest preserves stall and stock up while you can!

7 fl.oz vegetable oil
4 heaped tablespoons orange marmalade
6 oz caster sugar
3 large Manx free-range eggs
4 tablespoons Manx milk
6 oz wholewheat or wholemeal Manx Pioneer flour
6 oz Manx self-raising flour
½ teaspoon bicarbonate of soda

<u>For the topping:</u>
2 tablespoons orange marmalade
1 oz flaked almonds

Preheat the oven to 160°C. Place the oil, marmalade, sugar, eggs and milk into a large bowl and beat well with a wooden spoon. Gradually add the flour and bicarbonate of soda then mix again until well blended. Pour into a lined, 8" round baking tin and bake for 1½ hours. Test the cake with a skewer and if necessary bake for a further 10 minutes. Remove from the oven (but don't turn if off) and spread the remaining marmalade all over the cake then sprinkle with the almonds and return to the oven for 5 minutes.

"Try varying the type of marmalade you use to suit your taste. Go for thick, chunky peel if you like, or for something really different why not try lemon marmalade or rhubarb and ginger? The Laxey Fair, with its Victorian atmosphere, is usually a great place to find your favourites."

The Killip family

Butterscotch Choc Chip Biscuits

For the butterscotch sauce
45g light Muscovado sugar
2 tablespoons caster sugar
150g golden syrup
30g Manx butter
125ml Manx single cream
½ teaspoon vanilla extract

For the biscuits
250g lightly salted Manx butter
100g golden caster sugar
200g light brown Muscovado sugar
425g Manx self-raising flour
100g plain chocolate chips
2 tablespoons condensed milk
2 tablespoons butterscotch sauce

Pre-heat the oven to 150°C. Firstly make the butterscotch sauce by melting the sugars, syrup and butter in a saucepan. Turn up the heat and boil for 5 minutes. Add the cream and vanilla, stirring well, then take off the heat. Set aside and allow to cool slightly.

To make the biscuits, cream the butter and sugars then beat in the condensed milk, two tablespoons of butterscotch sauce and the chocolate chips. Gradually work in the flour to form a firmish dough. Take walnut-sized spoonfuls of the mixture and roll them into small balls. Place the balls on a baking tray, allowing room for spreading, and flatten them slightly with a fork. Bake for about ten minutes or until just golden. Place on a wire rack to cool (they will harden as they cool).

"Don't worry if you have more butterscotch sauce than you need - it keeps well in the fridge and is delicious warmed up and served over ice cream or a slice of ginger cake."

The Black family

Grantham Gingerbreads

Whether you've been rowing on Mooragh lake, climbing to the summit of South Barrule or walking through the tussock at the Ayres, these snappy ginger biscuits will always be welcomed by appetites sharpened in the fresh, Manx air.

100g Manx butter
350g caster sugar
1 medium Manx free-range egg,
   beaten
250g Manx self-raising flour
1 level teaspoon ground ginger

Makes about 30 biscuits

Image courtesy Barry Ogden

Point of Ayre

Pre-heat your oven to 150°C. Whisk the butter and sugar together in a large bowl until pale and fluffy. Gradually beat in the egg, then sift in the flour and ginger. Work the ingredients with a fork until the mixture forms a fairly firm dough. Roll the dough into walnut-sized balls and place each ball on a buttered baking sheet or sheet of baking parchment. Space well apart as they will spread while cooking. Bake in the oven for 40-45 minutes until crisp, well risen and lightly browned. They should sound hollow when tapped on the bottom. Remove to a wire rack and allow to cool thoroughly.

"We love walking and the Isle of Man is a haven for walkers, with miles of uninterrupted public footpaths, coastal tracks and winding glens. The views are stunning and it's amazing how quickly you can be in the heart of the countryside, with only birds and wildlife for company."

The Dimsdale family

Dundee Cake

This traditional fruit and almond cake may have its roots over the border - but there must be something magic about sharing a Celtic history as it also turns out beautifully when using good Manx ingredients!

6 oz Manx butter, softened
5 oz caster sugar
7 oz Manx self-raising flour
3 large Manx free-range eggs
2 oz mixed candied peel
4 oz sultanas
1 tablespoon sherry

1 tablespoon rum
1 oz ground almonds
4 oz currants
2 oz glace cherries
4 oz raisins
2 oz blanched halved almonds

Firstly, preheat your oven to 160°C and grease and line a 7-inch round cake tin with baking parchment. Combine the butter and sugar in a food processor until the mixture is light and fluffy then, keeping the machine running, add a third of the flour followed by one of the eggs and then the remaining flour and eggs. Stop the mixer and add the sherry, rum, dried fruit and ground almonds to the bowl then process again for just enough time to mix all the ingredients together. Pour the mixture into the baking tin and tap the tin to settle it, then sprinkle with the split almonds. Bake for about 2-2½ hours, or until a skewer inserted into the centre comes out clean (cover the top with a layer of damp greaseproof paper if it begins to brown before the end of cooking time).

"This recipe is from Sam's Scottish Nanny Agnes. Delicious and easy, it can be made just as well by hand"

The Turk family

Courgette Cake

This moist and very pretty cake - with its flecks of fruit, nuts and colour - is a great way to get children to eat vegetables! Dense, zingy and packed with flavour, it's a wonderful recipe for a summer afternoon tea in the garden.

3 large Manx free-range eggs
1 cup vegetable oil
2 cups Manx flour (1 wholemeal, 1 plain)
2 teaspoons baking powder
2 teaspoons bicarbonate of soda
2 teaspoons mixed spice
1 cup chopped dates
1 cup chopped nuts
1 cup dessicated coconut
2 cups soft brown sugar
2 large courgettes, grated
1 medium carrot, grated
2 teaspoons vanilla extract

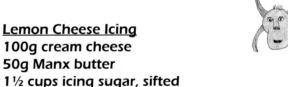

Lemon Cheese Icing
100g cream cheese
50g Manx butter
1½ cups icing sugar, sifted
Juice and zest of one lemon

Preheat the oven to 180°C. Beat the eggs with the vegetable oil till pale and creamy. In a large mixing bowl, sift the flour, baking powder, bicarb of soda and spice together then add the remaining ingredients and egg/ oil mixture and mix well. The mixture will be quite sloppy. Pour into a greased 23cm square cake tin (or two 1lb loaf tins) and bake for approx 45 mins or until a skewer comes out clean. Leave to cool in the tin (or tins).

To make the icing beat the cream cheese and butter together till smooth then gradually add the icing sugar, juice and zest and spread over the cooled cake.

The Read family

Carrot Cake

The humble carrot must be one of the most versatile vegetables there is - available all year round, grown right on our own doorstep and, best of all, can be eaten in a huge variety of ways, in soups, salads, casseroles, side dishes...and as the magic ingredient in this wonderfully moist cake.

For the cake:
8 oz Manx self-raising flour
2 teaspoons baking powder
5 oz soft brown sugar
2 oz walnuts, finely chopped (optional)
4 oz Manx carrots, peeled and grated
2 ripe bananas, mashed
2 large Manx free-range eggs
5 fl oz sunflower oil

For the topping:
6 oz full fat soft cheese
2 oz Manx butter, softened
4 oz icing sugar
A few drops vanilla essence or extract

Serves 8

Pre-heat your oven to 180°C. Grease and line an 8", deep cake tin. Place all the cake ingredients in a large mixing bowl and blend well with a hand mixer or wooden spoon until smooth. Pour into the cake tin and bake for 55 to 60 minutes until the cake is well risen and shrinking away from the sides. Remove from the oven and allow to cool in the tin for a few minutes before easing out onto a wire cake rack. To make the topping, place the soft cheese, butter, icing sugar and vanilla extract in a bowl and mix until smooth. Be careful not to overmix it or it will become runny.

Spread over the cooled cake and decorate, if you like, with walnut halves.

Chill slightly before serving and keep any leftovers in the fridge.

The Clague family

Mincemeat Slice

A nice sweet treat to serve up on Oie'll Voirrey or St Mary's Eve - the night before Christmas. The old Manx tradition of singing sacred ballads on this special night still survives today in small country chapels. Serve slices of this soft, fruity traybake with mugs of hot chocolate on your return home.

175g unsalted Manx butter, diced
75g golden caster sugar
150g Manx plain flour, sifted
1 teaspoon baking powder, sifted
100g ground almonds
4 medium Manx free-range eggs
400g mincemeat
150g fresh, uncooked cranberries
50g flaked almonds
75g glace cherries, roughly chopped
Icing sugar, for dusting

Image courtesy Barry Ogden
Groudle Glen

Pre-heat your oven to 170°C. Soften the butter and add the sugar, whisking lightly until light and fluffy. Add the eggs one at a time, mixing in each one. Add the flour, baking powder, ground almonds, mincemeat, cranberries, cherries, flaked almonds and blend well together. Pour into a deep square baking tray and smooth over. Bake for 35-40 mins until lightly golden and risen.

Allow to cool in the tin then cut into squares and serve.

The Linham family

Fudgy Chocolate Brownies

Sport plays a big part in Island life with hundreds of activities available - from athletics to kayaking, football to archery, and if you have an energetic family a treat like this at the end of the week is very welcome!

90g dark chocolate
150g unsalted Manx butter
125g plain Manx flour
15g cocoa powder
½ teaspoon baking powder
Pinch of salt
2 large Manx free-range eggs
300g soft light brown sugar
1 teaspoon vanilla extract
100g chopped walnuts (optional)   **Makes 12-16 brownies**

Preheat the oven to 180°C. Line the base of a 20 x 30cm shallow baking tin with non-stick baking parchment. Break the chocolate into a bowl and add the butter. Melt the mixture either by heating in the microwave for about one minute (checking and stirring every 20 seconds) or by heating in a bowl over a saucepan of simmering water. Remove the bowl and allow to cool slightly. Sieve the flour, cocoa powder, baking powder and salt into another bowl and in a third bowl beat the eggs with the sugar and vanilla until just combined. Using a large metal spoon, fold the chocolate mixture into the eggs then fold in the flour mixture (and nuts if using). Gently blend together only until the flour is no longer visible. Pour the mixture into the tin (it won't fill the tin but will spread out as it cooks) and bake for 20 minutes. When cooked it should be firm and slightly crispy on top and soft in the middle. Cool in the tin and cut into squares when cold.

"There are brownies - and then there are THESE brownies! Rich, dark, soft and fudgy centred. But remember, fold, don't stir for the perfect texture..."

Laxey Football Club

Banana Cake

In the old days a traditional Manx Tay would consist of fairly plain offerings such as oatcakes, sponge cakes and scones. Nowadays, however, 'exotic' fruits such as bananas are found in most kitchens allowing us to be much more adventurous with our teatime treats.

4 oz Manx butter, softened
6 oz soft brown sugar
2 Manx free-range eggs
8 oz Manx self-raising flour
3 ripe bananas
2 tablespoons Manx milk
1 teaspoon Bicarbonate of Soda

Preheat the oven to 200°C. In a large bowl, beat the butter and sugar together until light and fluffy. Add the eggs and mix well. In a separate bowl mash the bananas with a fork. Heat the milk until just boiling then stir in the bicarb of soda until dissolved and add to the mashed bananas. Add this mix to the egg, sugar and butter mixture and stir well. Fold in the flour and spoon into either 2 greased sandwich tins or 2 x 1lb loaf tins. Bake for 45 minutes if using the loaf tins or 35 minutes if using the sandwich tins. When well risen and brown on top, remove to a wire rack to cool completely before removing from the tins.

If using the sandwich tins, spread one of the cakes with fresh whipped cream and sliced bananas and place the other cake on top. Serve straightaway.

If making loaves, these can be securely wrapped and frozen to use at a later date.

"This recipe comes from Great-Grandad and Nana Duggan. Great Grandad was one of the first children to go to Laxey School, which has now had four generations of the family there. The recipe has been a firm family favourite since we were first married and has never failed us yet".

The Burgess family

Rock Buns

These nostalgic teatime treats are guaranteed to induce feelings of pure pleasure.

12 oz Manx self-raising flour
6 oz sugar
A pinch of salt
¼ teaspoon nutmeg
¼ teaspoon mixed spice
6 oz Manx butter, softened

3 oz currants (or mixed dried fruit - whatever you have)
1 ½ oz chopped peel (optional - use more dried fruit instead if you prefer)
1 large Manx free-range egg, beaten
A dash of Manx whole-cream milk to mix

Pre-heat your oven to 200°C. Sieve the flour, salt and spices together into a large bowl. Rub in the butter, then add the sugar, fruit and peel (if using). Mix in the beaten egg and enough milk to bind the mixture into a soft dough, making sure not to overmix. Using a teaspoon and a fork, place rock-shaped heaps of the mixture on a greased baking sheet and bake for 15-20 minutes until risen and golden brown.

"This is my mum's recipe from the 1950's and it's still going strong. Scarlett, Matilda and their cousins have all made these with grandma over the years! We tend to make it in triple or quadruple batches."

The Clague family

Flapjacks

1 lb porridge oats
8 oz golden syrup

8 oz Manx butter
4 oz demerara sugar

Pre-heat your oven to 170°C. Gently heat the sugar, butter and golden syrup until melted. Leave to cool slightly then add the oats and mix well together. Spread the mixture on to a shallow baking tray and bake for 25 - 30 minutes till golden brown. Allow to cool in the tin then slice into squares.

The Moffat family

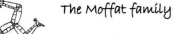

Gran's Fifteens

15 Digestive biscuits, crushed
15 glacé cherries, cut in half
15 marshmallows,
   chopped into small pieces

15 walnuts, finely chopped
15 milk chocolate drops
50 grams dessicated coconut
½ large can condensed milk

Pour the condensed milk into a large bowl. Add all the dry ingredients and mix well. Tip out onto a clean working surface and, using your hands, roll into a long 'sausage' shape. Sprinkle the coconut onto the worktop and roll the 'sausage' in the coconut until it is evenly coated. Wrap in tin foil and place in the fridge for about one hour. Remove the foil and slice into one-inch thick rounds. Place each round in a paper case to serve.

"I love this recipe because they are yummy and I can make them myself"
Max Turner (Laxey School)

Vanilla Cake

3 oz lightly salted Manx butter, softened
1 cup soft light brown sugar
1¼ cups self-raising Manx flour
2 large Manx free-range eggs, lightly beaten
½ cup Manx milk
1 teaspoon baking powder
2 teaspoons vanilla extract

<u>For the icing</u>
1 cup icing sugar
1 tablespoon cold water
1 teaspoon vanilla extract

Serves 8

Pre-heat the oven to 180°C. Place the butter and brown sugar in a large bowl and mix well. Sift the flour and baking powder into the butter mixture, then add the eggs, milk and vanilla and mix with an electric whisk for three minutes till pale and creamy. Pour into a greased, round baking tin and bake for 30 - 35 minutes. Allow to cool in the tin. Make the icing by blending the water and vanilla with the icing sugar until it is smooth and thick. Spread over the cake and decorate with sprigs of fresh Manx lavender.

"I have always enjoyed cooking with my Mum and this is the first cake I made by myself" Alexandra King (Laxey School)

Gluten Free Crunchy Ginger Biscuits

A lovely, simple but tasty biscuit with great texture. Perfect for hungry children after school.

100g medium oatmeal or oat bran
100g gluten free flour
50g sugar
½ teaspoon bicarbonate of soda
1-2 teaspoons ground ginger
100g Manx butter
1 tablespoon Manx milk
1 level tablespoon golden syrup or honey

Pre-heat your oven to 150°C. Place the first five ingredients in a bowl and mix well. In a small saucepan heat the remaining ingredients together until melted but not too hot. Pour the liquid into the bowl of dry ingredients and mix well to form a dough. Roll into a long sausage shape and divide into approx 24 equal sized pieces. Roll each piece into a small ball, flatten a little and place on greased baking sheets, giving them enough room to spread as they cook.

Bake for about 25 minutes until golden brown. Check them after 20 minutes to ensure they don't overcook or they'll taste bitter. Place the baking sheets on a rack to cool for 15 minutes. The biscuits will firm up as they cool.

'These are great biscuits to experiment with. For instance, you could try using porridge oats to give a different texture or add 4 or 5 pieces of finely chopped crystallised ginger for a hint of 'warmth'. You can also use ordinary flour instead of gluten free. Most recipes can be adapted - it's just a case of try it and see!'

The Taylor family

Sam's Mars Bar Chocolate Crispie Crunch

Simple to make, but oh so more-ish... This is a treat you'd do anything for! Sam's visit to Laxey School was an inspiration to all her young fans.

Image courtesy Isle of Man Newspapers

Sam Barks at the Isle of Man TT Races

75g Manx butter
2 standard size Mars Bars
230g (big block) milk chocolate
100g rice crispies

Melt the Mars Bars and butter together - you can do this in the microwave in a microwave-proof bowl or on the hob over another pan of boiling water. When the mixture is melted, stir well and carefully mix in the rice crispies. Line a 200mm x 50mm deep baking tray with non-stick foil and spoon the mixture into the tin and spread it evenly. Melt the large bar of milk chocolate (same method as earlier) and evenly pour over the rice crispie mixture. Place in the fridge to set and while it's cooling, lick the spoon - the best part of the process, I think!

Once the crispie crunch is ready, cut into squares and enjoy!

This recipe kindly donated by Samantha Barks, former Laxey School pupil, singing sensation, finalist in the BBC hit series 'I'd Do Anything' and star of 'Cabaret' alongside Wayne Sleep.

Sam says "I don't consider myself to be much of a cook but I do enjoy making what I like to eat and this is one of my favourites! I used to make it with my big sister Kim - it's really simple to make, great for parties or just good fun."

Tiffin

The original meaning of the word 'tiffin' is a light meal but these days we think of it more as a treat for morning or afternoon tea. This no-cook chocolate slice is perfect for either and is a great way of using up the assorted biscuits at the bottom of the biscuit barrel. Just remember to start it the day before you need it...

4 oz Manx butter, softened
1 tablespoon golden syrup
1 dessertspoon cocoa powder
2 dessertpoons drinking chocolate
1 dessertspoon caster sugar
8 oz plain biscuits

For the topping:
8 oz milk or dark chocolate (according to taste)
A splash of Manx milk
A chunk of Manx butter

In a saucepan melt the butter, syrup, cocoa powder, drinking chocolate and sugar over a gentle heat till blended together. Remove from the heat and set aside. Place the biscuits in a large plastic bag and bash with a rolling pin until the consistency of breadcrumbs. Pour the crumbs into the syrup mixture, stir well then spoon into a shallow greased baking tin. Place in the fridge overnight.

The following day melt the topping ingredients together then, using a spatula, smooth the mixture over the chilled biscuit base. Return to the fridge to set before cutting into squares.

Friends of Christ Church, Laxey - 'Coffee and Chat' Group.
Open to all, every Thursday 10-12

MISCELLANEOUS

If you're simply wanting to pack a picnic and head to a picturesque Manx beach for the day, just reach for a jar of homemade chutney, some warm, fresh bread, a fruity drink and something sweet to finish...and you have a perfect taste of the Isle of Man.

Agatoag Beetroot (Sweet and Sour Beetroot)

Summertime in the Island - walks in the sand dunes at the Ayres, long sunsets at Niarbyl, shark-spotting at Peel - and the joys of fresh local vegetables in salads or side dishes. This unusual use of beetroot makes an interesting alternative to red cabbage and tastes great with grilled Manx pork sausages.

2 lbs fresh Manx beetroot
2 Manx onions, finely chopped
1½ oz Manx butter
1½ oz Manx plain flour
2 beef stock cubes dissolved in ¾ pint water
4 tablespoons malt vinegar
1-2 tablespoons brown sauce
2 tablespoons sugar
1 level teaspoon French mustard

Serves 4

Wash, top and tail the beetroot but try not to cut the flesh. Leave the skin and boil them in a large pan of salted water until tender (large beetroot take 45-60mins, smaller ones about 30 mins). Leave to cool then put on some rubber gloves and gently rub the skin off the beetroots and cut the flesh into chunks. Melt the butter in a large frying pan and gently fry the onions until golden brown. Mix in the flour then slowly add the stock and bring to the boil, stirring all the time. Add the other ingredients and the cooked beetroot and gently simmer for 20 minutes. Serve as a side dish with grilled meat and mashed potatoes.

"This recipe's unusual name was made up by my grandson George. I have no idea what the word means or why he thought of it, but since then it has always been, and shall always remain, Agatoag Beetroot."

Jane Ratcliffe

Old Doverhouse Chutney

Plums are plentiful in the Isle of Man in late Summer/ early Autumn, not only from fruit growers and markets but in the wild! The wooded valleys of Laxey are especially gifted with plum trees - in the Spring, look out for their beautiful blossom while riding on the tram. The Island's clean air and lack of pollution also makes it a haven for wild sloes, blackberries, hazelnuts, bilberries, elderberries, chestnuts, mushrooms and chanterelles. Just grab a basket and get picking...

1½ lb fresh Manx plums, stones removed and quartered
1½ lb Manx cooking apples (weight after peeling)
8 oz Manx green or red tomatoes, skinned and chopped
1 lb raisins
8 oz Manx onions, peeled and finely chopped
1½ lb demerara sugar
4 oz preserved ginger, chopped
1 clove garlic, finely chopped
1 whole red chilli, seeds removed and finely chopped
1½ tablespoons salt
1 pint malt vinegar

Image courtesy Allison Ratcliffe
Isle of Man Steam Railway

Place all the ingredients into a very large, heavy bottomed saucepan, stir well then bring to the boil. Lower the heat and simmer very gently (just 'plopping' slightly), uncovered, for about one and a half hours or until the mixture is thick. Stir frequently towards the end of the cooking time to prevent the chutney sticking and burning. Allow to cool slightly then pot into warm sterilized jars and cover with waxed discs and cellophane covers. When cool, label and place in a dark store cupboard for three months to mature (though it will taste even better if you have the patience to leave it for up to a year!). Serve with strong Manx cheddar or Red Leicester cheese and oatmeal crackers.

"This is a wonderful recipe for using up excess fruit and vegetables at the end of the summer. Just remember to leave open all your doors and windows while it's simmering and don't be tempted to rush it - long, slow cooking is the secret to really good chutney!"

John Wood, Laxey Woollen Mill

Old Fashioned Lemonade

Home-made lemonade was the highlight of many a Manx tearoom menu during the early twentieth century, when thousands of tourists flocked to the Isle of Man for their summer holidays. Laxey's Ham and Egg Terrace, which tourists passed by on their way to visit the famous Laxey Wheel, even gained its name from such tearooms. Recreate those halcyon days of old with this simple recipe.

3 large lemons (preferably unwaxed organic lemons)
6 oz white sugar
1½ pints boiling water

Wash the lemons and finely grate the rind. Place the rind with the sugar into a basin and pour over the boiling water. Cover and leave to cool, stirring occasionally. Add the juice of the lemons and then strain into a large lidded jug. Cover and place in the fridge until needed then serve in tall glasses with ice and a sprig of fresh mint.

The Pycroft family

Manx Summer Smoothies

Smoothies are a wonderful way to make the most of soft fruits such as strawberries and raspberries - abundant in the Isle of Man from June to August. Or why not try fresh Manx blackberries and stewed apple, or stewed Manx rhubarb and honey?

6 fl. oz full-fat Manx milk
1 teaspoon clear Manx honey
Large handful of fresh or frozen Manx summer berries
1 tablespoon Manx vanilla ice cream or plain yoghurt

Place all the ingredients into a blender (or use a hand blender and large jug). Whizz for 30 seconds until smooth then pour into a tall glass and drink straightaway. Simple, nutritious and delicious!

The Emms family - Laxey Post Office

Poppy Seed Beer Bread

The yeast in the beer means there's no need to add extra baking yeast to this recipe and the only kneading required is done before it goes in the oven. The beer gives it a lovely, dark, slightly sweet flavour.

5 cups Manx bread flour
1 teaspoon salt
1 litre Manx beer
Manx butter for greasing
1 tablespoon poppy seeds   **Makes 1 large loaf**

Firstly, sift the flour and salt into a large mixing bowl. Gradually pour in the beer and mix until the dough is very stiff and comes away from the sides of the bowl. Cover with a teatowel and set aside for an hour in a warm place (an airing cupboard is ideal). Preheat your oven to 220°C and grease a deep 2lb loaf or cake tin with butter and dust with flour. By now the dough should have doubled in size so tip it out onto a floured board, punch it down and knead for 10 minutes until smooth and elastic. Place in the baking tin, sprinkle with the poppy seeds and bake at the very high heat for 15 minutes then reduce the heat to 200°C and bake for a further 30 minutes.

When the bread is cooked it should sound hollow when tapped on the bottom.

Eat while still warm with chunks of mature Manx cheese and onion relish.

"Good bread relies on using the right ingredients for the job and we've found that either Manx Queen strong white bread flour or Traditional Manx Wholemeal Flour give the best results. Plus of course the purity of Okell's beer gives the loaf that extra 'x factor'!"
The Bearman family

Lemon Curd

Home-made lemon curd is quite simply sublime. Rich, sweet, tangy and unctuous it is glorious eaten simply on lightly buttered bread or used in desserts such as Laxey Meringue Mess (see Desserts p54). A jar of freshly made lemon curd always makes a special gift - friends and loved ones will definitely thank you for it!

Grated rind and juice of 4 lemons
4 large Manx free-range eggs, beaten
4 oz Manx butter
12 oz caster sugar

Image courtesy Barry Ogden

Laxey Woollen Mill

Place all the ingredients in a large glass heatproof bowl and sit it over a pan of gently simmering water. Stir continuously with a wooden spoon until the sugar has dissolved and the butter has melted, then continue stirring for about 20 minutes until the curd has thickened. It is very important that you don't allow the mix to boil or it will curdle.

Pour into warm sterilized jars, seal and allow to cool then store in the fridge.

As the curd contains eggs it should be eaten within a few days.

"This is a little time consuming but I plan ahead and make sure I have something to do while stirring - place a magazine at a convenient but safe distance from the hob, have a book on hand or make some phone calls to friends to pass the time. It is worth the effort though and is one of the simplest lemon curd recipes ever."

Jane Ratcliffe

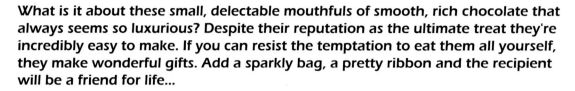

Heavenly Truffles

What is it about these small, delectable mouthfuls of smooth, rich chocolate that always seems so luxurious? Despite their reputation as the ultimate treat they're incredibly easy to make. If you can resist the temptation to eat them all yourself, they make wonderful gifts. Add a sparkly bag, a pretty ribbon and the recipient will be a friend for life...

For the truffles:
200g chocolate (milk, dark or plain)
100ml Manx double cream
25g liquid glucose (liquid glucose acts a preservative. With it the truffles will keep for 6 weeks, without they will keep for 1 week)

For the flavourings (optional, and according to taste)
Rum, brandy or cinnamon (if using dark chocolate)
Cointreau, Baileys or Grand Marnier (if using milk chocolate)
Vanilla extract (if using white chocolate)

For the coating:
Cocoa powder, icing sugar, caster sugar, chopped roasted nuts, toasted dessicated coconut or even more melted chocolate

Chop up the chocolate, place in a large bowl and microwave on full power in 20-30 second bursts, stirring after each burst to distribute the heat. Repeat until the chocolate is melted. In a small saucepan heat the cream and glucose to boiling point and pour over the melted chocolate. Stir thoroughly. If you want to flavour the truffles add a little of the suggested ingredients, tasting until you achieve the intensity you want. Leave to firm up but not harden (don't be tempted to put it in the fridge unless it's the middle of summer). Once the texture is firm, roll into a sausage shape (you may need to dust the roll with cocoa powder). Cut into even sized pieces and roll each into a ball. Cover each ball in your preferred coating. Set aside to firm up then place in a cellophane gift bag or small box and keep in a cool place.

The Crawford family

Eastern Young Farmers' Fudge

If you can resist the temptation to eat this all yourself it makes a lovely gift. Cut it into small squares and wrap in individual cellophane bags tied with ribbon.

1 lb sugar
¼ lb Manx butter
¼ pint fresh Manx milk
1 tablespoon golden syrup
200g condensed milk
½ teaspoon vanilla extract

Image courtesy Ed Clague

Eastern Young Farmers

Place the butter and milk in a saucepan and melt slowly. Add the rest of the ingredients and bring to a steady boil, stirring continuously for 35 minutes. Leave for 5 minutes, then put the saucepan in a shallow sink of cool water and beat the mixture with a wooden spoon until it begins to set. Spoon out into a shallow dish and mark into squares. Allow to set thoroughly before cutting into pieces.

This recipe kindly donated by the Eastern Young Farmers. The hillside mural on the back cover is some of their handiwork. These hard-working young people are also great entertainers and supporters of local charities. Their annual concerts are legendary!

English - Manx Glossary of Cookery Terms Used in This Book
Kindly translated by Chris Sheard, Manx Heritage Foundation

A
Almonds - Almonyn
Apple - Ooyl

B
Bake - Fuinney
Baked Beans - Poanraghyn fuinnit
Baking Tin - Stainney fuinnee
Banana - Corran bwee
Barley - Oarn
Basil - Bassyl
Baste (v) - Bastal
Bay leaf - Duillag laurys
Beans - Poanraghyn
Beef - Feill-vart
Beer - Lhune
Beetroot - Beetys
Blend (v.) - Covestey
Boil - Broie
Bowl -Meilley
Bread - Arran
Breadcrumbs - Kinneigyn arran
Burger - Burgeyr
Butter - Eeym
Butterscotch - Taffee eeymey

C
Cabbage - Caayl
Can opener - Fosleyder stainney
Carrot - Carradje
Casserole - Casseroil
Cauliflower - Collag
Celery - Smullish
Cheese - Caashey
Cherry - Shillish
Chicken - Feill-chirkey
Chickpeas - Pishyr chirkey
Chill (v) - Feayraghey
Chilli - Çhillee
Chives - Shoushan
Chocolate - Shocklaid
Chop - Asney (n); Scoltey (v)
Chutney - Çhutnee

Cider - Lhune ooyl
Cinnamon - Cannial
Cocoa - Coco
Coconut - Cro bainney
Cold - Feayr
Cook (v & n) - Coagyrey
Crab - Partan
Crust - Scroig
Cup - Cappan
Curry - Curree

D
Date - Date
Delicious - Ard-vlastal
Dine - Goaill jinnair
Dinner - Jinnair
Dish - Jyst
Dough - Teayst arran

E
Eat - Gee
Eggs - Oohyn
Enjoy - Goaill soylley

F
Flour - Flooyr
Fork - Aall
Freeze - Riojey
Fridge - Kishtey-rio
Fry - Freeghey

G
Gammon - Gamboon
Garlic - Garleid
Garnish - Jesheen
Ginger - Jinshar
Gram - Gram
Grape - Berrish-feeyney
Grate (v) - Screebey
Grease (v) - Smarrey
Grill (v) - Greddaney
Grind - Blieh

H
Ham - Yskid
Heat - Çhiow (v), Çhiass (n)
Herbs - Lossreeyn blasstal
Herring - Skeddan
Honey - Mill
Horseradish - Rahgyl

Hot - Çheh

I
Ice cream - Key riojit
Icing - Riojaghey
Ingredient - Mynayrn

J
Jelly - Gleiy
Juice - Soo

K
Kidney - Aarey
Kilogram - Kilogram
Kipper - Skeddan jiarg
Knife - Skynn

L
Lamb - Feill-eayn
Leek - Cannian
Lemonade - Limonaid
Lentil - Pishyr lughag
Lime - Limon glass

M
Main course - Coorse mooar
Marmalade - Marmalaid
Mash - (v) Lahney
Meat - Feill
Meringue - Fynnicane
Microwave - Oghe meegra-honn
Milk - Bainney
Mincemeat - Myn-eill
Mushroom - Shalmane

N
Nuts - Croyn

O
Oatmeal - Meinn chorkey
Oats - Corkey
Offal - Bee brisht
Oil - Ooill
Onion - Unnish
Orange - Noirid
Ounce - Awnse
Oven - Oghe
Oven gloves - Laueanyn oghe

P
Parsley - Parsal
Pasta - Pastey
Paste - Teayst
Peach - Pershagh
Peanut - Cro thallooin
Pears - Peearyn
Peas - Pishyryn
Peel (v) - Speeiney
Pie - Pye
Pineapple - Nannys
Pint - Pynt
Pizza - Peetsey
Plum - Plumbys
Potato - Praase
Pound - Punt
Prawns - Praneyn
Pudding Puiddin
Pumpkin - Pumkin

Q
Quantity - Mooadys
Queenies - Roaganyn beggey

R
Raisins - Raisinyn
Recipe - Aght-aarlee
Redcurrant - Berrish yiarg
Rhubarb - Rubarb
Rice - Reesh
Rind - Speeineig
Roast (v) - Rostey

S
Sage - Creaghlagh
Salmon - Braddan
Salt - Sollan
Sauce - Aunlyn
Saucepan - Skillad
Sausage - Pronnag
Scallops - Roaganyn
Scone - Sconnag
Season (v) - Cur Irreeagh
Separate - Scarrey
Serve - Cur er boayrd
Shred - Mynyiarrey
Sieve - Creear

Simmer - Fo-vroie
Skin - Crackan
Slice - Shlissag
Soda - Soda
Soup - Awree
Spatula - Spaddyl
Spice - Spios
Spoon - Spein
Sprinkle - Skeaylley
Starter - Coorse toshee
Steam (v) - Gaalvroie
Stew - Brouish
Stir - Seiy
Stock - Sthock
Sugar - Shugyr
Swede - Napin bwee

T
Tablespoon - Spein buird
Teaspoon - Spein tey
Terrine - Terreen
Thyme - Çheeim
Tin - Stainney
Toast - Arran greddanit
Toaster - Greddaner
Tomato - Ooyl-ghraih
Treacle - Treegyl
Turkey - Kiark rangagh
Turnip - Napin

V
Vanilla - Vanilley
Vegetable - Losserey
Vegetarian - Lossreyder
Vinegar - Feeyn geayr

W
Warm - Blah
Watercress - Burley
Wheat - Curnaght
Whisk - Blinkeyder
Wine - Feeyn
Wooden spoon - Spein fuygh

Y
Yoghurt - Binjean-villish